TRAVELLERS

MEDITERRANEAN CRUISING

By
DEBBIE STOWE

Written by Debbie Stowe
Original photography by Vasile Szakacs

Published by Thomas Cook Publishing
A division of Thomas Cook Tour Operations Limited.
Company registration no. 3772199 England
The Thomas Cook Business Park, Unit 9, Coningsby Road,
Peterborough PE3 8SB, United Kingdom
E-mail: books@thomascook.com, Tel: + 44 (0) 1733 416477
www.thomascookpublishing.com

Produced by Cambridge Publishing Management Limited
Burr Elm Court, Main Street, Caldecote CB23 7NU

ISBN: 978-1-84848-093-3

Text © 2009 Thomas Cook Publishing
Maps © 2009 Thomas Cook Publishing/PCGraphics (UK) Limited

Series Editor: Maisie Fitzpatrick
Production/DTP: Steven Collins

Printed and bound in Italy by Printer Trento

Cover photography: Front L–R: © PSI/Alamy; © Ripani Massimo/4CR;
© William Manning/Alamy
Back: © Giovanni Simeone/4CR

Contents

Introduction

With the sea breeze in your hair, azure waters as far as the eye can see and a plethora of fascinating ports to explore, cruising has been the holiday of choice for the well-heeled for over a century. Incorporating ports as diverse as Monte Carlo and Menorca, Venice and Valletta, a Mediterranean cruise consists of parts of Europe, Africa and Asia, distilled and served up in the most convenient and palatable form.

Cruising is still popular among the super-wealthy (although oligarchs, business tycoons and superstars tend to prefer the privacy of their own yachts rather than slumming it with the general public), but it is no longer their sole preserve. Thanks to falling holiday prices and the entrance of low-cost

The coastline of the Côte d'Azur

operators, Mediterranean jaunts now start at the price of a good-value traditional package holiday. This has also opened up the market to a younger demographic, meaning cruising has shed its reputation as a 'grey' getaway.

The advantages of a cruise are manifest. You've got all the variety of a road trip, and can easily cover hundreds, sometimes thousands, of kilometres, taking in three or four countries in a week. All of this is achieved without the hassle of repeated packing and unpacking, driving and trawling for hotels. Rather than raising your blood pressure over map-reading errors and foreign road tolls, your journey time can be spent relaxing on deck. You know in advance exactly what to expect – and what you'll spend. Choose your ship carefully and you'll also have all leisure needs met, from the casino to yoga to dancing all night.

But of course, the chief draw for many are the ports and sights themselves. The 2.5 million sq km (965,000sq miles) of

A cruise ship in the harbour at Mykonos

water that make up the Mediterranean Sea take you to some of the most fascinating towns of three continents. Culturally, Istanbul and Rome are hard to beat, while history buffs can explore Athens and Alexandria. For glamour and bling, there's the Côte d'Azur, while art and architecture lovers have Florence and Barcelona. Sun-seekers, meanwhile, will be sated in Greece and Turkey. While some of the region's classic tourist destinations, such as Venice, will be on the itinerary, a Mediterranean cruise often deposits the traveller in a lesser-known spot, such as Split or Dubrovnik, so introducing you to a destination you might not have thought of visiting by yourself.

The abundance of cities that can feature also gives rise to a gastronomic smorgasbord, from the famed pizza and pasta of Italy, to tapas in Spain, fine French fare and the spicier cuisines south of the region. And the peoples you will encounter upon disembarking will be equally varied and fascinating, from chic French women with tiny dogs to gnarled Greek fishermen. Meanwhile, the togetherness of the ship atmosphere makes it easy to forge friendships with like-minded voyagers.

Though the whistle-stop nature of the typical cruise can make you yearn to have longer in some of the ports, a Mediterranean cruise offers an affordable, enjoyable and easy introduction to a cornucopia of great places – and all with a touch of old-world glamour.

The region

Such a vast region is impossible to compress into a few adjectives. A Mediterranean cruise and its attendant excursions can take in African deserts, large European metropolises, sleepy Greek islands, sophisticated resorts and workaday ports. Politically, the differences are no less stark, with the liberal and progressive democracies of some of the European Union states juxtaposed with the more autocratic, traditional regimes to the east and south.

For the purposes of this book, the region has been divided along approximate cultural and geographical lines. The section on Iberia and the Balearics includes Spain, which enjoys one of the most varied geographies in Europe. Mountains, plains and beaches follow hot on each other's heels. What is not so wide-ranging, thankfully, is the weather – in summer the sunshine is pretty much as guaranteed as it can ever be in this corner of the world. Both a Spanish province and an autonomous community in their own right, the Balearic Islands are an archipelago dominated by two main islands, Mallorca and Menorca. Catalan is an official language here, alongside Spanish. The islands share the mixed geography of the mainland, with hills, plateaux and lowlands.

Portugal, too, is included in this section. Despite not bordering the Mediterranean – its beaches are framed instead by the Atlantic Ocean – it still features on cruise itineraries in the region, often on those that start in the UK. The country's southern reaches are marked by rolling plains, and share the enviable climate of neighbouring Spain. This section of the book is completed by Gibraltar, which is (controversially) a British overseas territory, despite sharing a northern border with Spain. This southwestern tip of Europe is well known for the Rock of Gibraltar, a monolithic limestone promontory. One of the world's most densely populated territories, one tenth of Gibraltar consists of reclaimed land. Both Spain and Portugal are part of the European Union, and, as a British territory, so is Gibraltar, although it has exemptions from some aspects of EU law.

The second section can be thought of as the heart of the Med. It was medieval Italy that spawned the term 'Riviera', and today the French and Italian versions are most associated with the word and all its associations of warm weather and good coastal living. The south of France (nicknamed *Le Midi*) is

The region

RUSSIAN FEDERATION
UKRAINE
Donets'k
MOLDOVA
CHISINAU
Chisinau International
Odessa
Sevastopol
Black Sea
Samsun
Sivas
Ankara-Esenboga International
ANKARA
TURKEY
Adana
Aleppo
SYRIA
DAMASCUS
AMMAN
JORDAN
BEIRUT
LEBANON
NICOSIA
CYPRUS
JERUSALEM
ISRAEL
Cairo International
CAIRO
Giza
EGYPT
Alexandria
Benghazi
LIBYA

Konya
Antalya
Marmaris
Rhodes
Kos
Bodrum
Ephesus
Izmir
Balikesir
Bursa
Istanbul-Atatürk
Istanbul
Zonguldak
Dobrich
Constanta
Galati
Bucharest International
BUCHAREST
Banésa
ROMANIA
Chisinau International

SLOVAKIA
Bratislava-Mnt Stefánik
BRATISLAVA
BUDAPEST
HUNGARY
CZECH REPUBLIC
GERMANY
Munich
VIENNA
Vienna International
AUSTRIA
ZAGREB
SLOVENIA
LJUBLJANA
CROATIA
Belgrade-Nikola Tesla
BELGRADE
SERBIA
B & H
SARAJEVO
Sarajevo International
BULGARIA
SOFIA
SKOPJE
MACEDONIA
PRISTINA
MONT.
PODGORICA
TIRANA
ALBANIA
KOS
Thessaloniki
Aegean Sea
GREECE
ATHENS
Athens International
Patras
Mykonos
Syros
Paros
Kalymnos
Kos
Crete
Tripoli

Zante
Kefalonia
Corfu
Ionian Sea
Messina
Sicily
Pompeii
Naples
Palermo
Tyrrhenian Sea
Cagliari
Sardinia
Ajaccio
Corsica
St-Tropez
Cannes
Nice
MONACO
Livorno
Pisa
Florence
Genoa
Turin
Milan
Venice
Split
Dubrovnik
ROME
Rome-Ciampino
Civitavecchia
ITALY

Valletta
MALTA
TRIPOLI
Tripoli International
Gabès
TUNIS
Tunis-Carthage International
TUNISIA
Sfax

Mediterranean Sea

FRANCE
PARIS
Paris-Charles De Gaulle
Tours
Nantes
Limoges
Lyon
Bordeaux
Toulouse
Marseille
Toulon
BERN
Bern Belp
SWITZERLAND
Zurich
PORTUGAL
LISBON
Lisbon-Portela
Portimão
Cádiz
Gibraltar (UK)
Tangier
Casablanca
RABAT
Rabat-Salé
Salé
MOROCCO
Oujda
Tlemcen
Oran
ALGIERS
Algiers-Houari Boumedienne
ALGERIA
SPAIN
MADRID
Madrid-Barajas International
Toledo
Albacete
Seville
Málaga
Marbella
Valencia
Zaragoza
Barcelona
Menorca
Mallorca
Palma
Ibiza
Balearic Islands
Bilbao
Valladolid
Oviedo
Bay of Biscay

N

Large City
Small City
Large Town
Airport

0 300km
0 150 miles

synonymous with viticulture, languorous villages (beloved of British second-homers) and the chic Côte d'Azur. Italy's distinctive boot shape confers on it a generous proportion of coastline, and as a result many of its most important towns are on, or within easy reach of, the coast. Close to Italy but in fact entirely enclosed by France is the tiny tax haven, Monaco.

For a taste of France or Italy with a twist, the islands of Corsica, Sardinia and Sicily each have their own distinctive cultures and landscapes. Although it is closer to Italy, Corsica is a French region. Its renown comes from its status as the birthplace of Napoleon; the island is comprised largely of a single mountain range and boasts over 200 beaches. Similarly mountainous, the Italian island of Sardinia is separated from Corsica by the Strait of Bonifacio. Sicily (whose name derives from its triangular shape) is the biggest island in the Mediterranean. It is home to Mount Etna, the largest active volcano in Europe (though it is perhaps better known for its similarly volatile Mafia associations).

Both Italy and France, plus their islands, are part of the European Union, although the political situation

A painting of an ancient map of the Mediterranean on display at the Museum of Underwater Archaeology in Bodrum, Turkey

A view of Mount Etna from Taormina, Sicily

in the region is not without controversy. Many Corsicans want greater autonomy from France (with a minority even calling for independence), and similar political currents can be found in Sicily. Italian politics in general have been colourful, to say the least, with frequent regime changes and corruption scandals.

Moving eastwards, the next section comprises a relative newcomer to most travellers' holiday radars, the Dalmatian Coast, and the more traditional destinations of Greece and Turkey. Dalmatia's two main cruise ports, separated from eastern Italy by the Adriatic Sea, are Split and Dubrovnik, both in Croatia. However, the coastline's numerous islands, coves and channels, plus on-shore national parks,

suggest that in the future, when the area's associations with political upheaval have faded, more of its destinations may make it onto the map. Formerly part of Yugoslavia, Croatia is now a candidate country for European Union membership. Further south, Greece and Turkey are well known to holidaymakers for their glorious weather and miles of sandy beach. Both are also rich in historical attractions. While Greece has the jewel in the crown for holidaymakers with its islands, discrete specks of dazzling colours, Turkey's landscape holds its own, with imposing mountains and aridly impressive countryside that seems unchanged from biblical times.

Greece's economy has prospered since the country became part of the

A scene typical of the Greek islands, here at Paros

European Union, and managed to avoid the tension and violence that beset its fellow Balkan states. Across the Aegean Sea, Turkey is another potential EU member (despite the fact that the majority of its landmass lies inside Asia). Although the majority of the country's population is nominally Muslim, Turkey is fiercely secular. A controversy – and sticking point on Turkey's EU membership path – is the issue of Cyprus, an independent state and EU member whose northern reaches are claimed by Turkey (although no other country recognises the claim). Like the Greek islands in the region, golden sands and great weather have imprinted Cyprus on the tourist trail.

Political instability is greater in the countries covered by the final section of this book, the south, comprising the North African countries on the southern shores of the Mediterranean, from Egypt in the east to Morocco in the west. The gateway between Asia and Africa, any mention of Egypt immediately calls to mind deserts, dust and sand dunes, along with the astonishing symbols of ancient Egypt such as pharaohs, pyramids and sphinxes. Politically, the president is a formidable figure. Multi-candidate presidential elections have recently been introduced, but at the moment the chance of a challenger ousting the incumbent remains theoretical.

It's a similar story in several of the North African states. Tunisia's president is also a highly authoritative individual, and his photograph adorns public places in a manner that would seem absurdly deferential across the other side of the Mediterranean. Morocco's king (formerly a sultan) has a similarly influential role. In Algeria, too, power is bound up largely in the presidency, although with just a decade in office under his belt, the incumbent is a relative newcomer compared to his counterparts in Egypt and Tunisia.

Physically, North Africa's Mediterranean coast has much in common with the geography of the European side. The Atlas Mountains are part of the same fold mountain system that runs through Southern Europe. Olives and citrus fruits are among the crops that grow in the region, although further south the desert reduces the fecundity. Indeed, the Mediterranean Basin is often loosely defined as the Old World region where olive trees grow.

Though it doesn't fit neatly into any grouping, Malta has been included here for largely geographical reasons. The archipelago nation consists of three large inhabited islands, Malta Island,

Gozo and Comino, and several smaller uninhabited ones. Though technically European, the country lies on the border of the African tectonic plate and the Eurasian plate, although the belief that it is Europe's southernmost point is mistaken – that spot is on a Greek island. Malta's landscape consists mainly of low hills and neat fields. The country's political system borrows significantly from Westminster, and unlike the row of countries to the south, the president is for the most part a ceremonial head of state.

Presidential authority is strong in North African countries: here, a portrait of Tunisia's president in a corridor between flats

History

50 million years ago The Mediterranean Sea is formed through continental drift.

4th millennium BC Civilisation first develops in Mesopotamia and spreads to the east coast of the Mediterranean.

8th century BC Earliest Greek alphabetic inscriptions emerge.

814 BC Carthage founded in North Africa. In a little over a century the Carthaginians establish strongholds in Italy, Sicily and Sardinia.

776 BC Ancient Olympic Games first staged.

753 BC Legend has it that twins Romulus and Remus found Rome in this year.

5th–4th centuries BC Classical period of Ancient Greece, ending with the death of Alexander the Great in 323 BC, who had conquered the eastern Mediterranean from Egypt to Greece.

5th–1st centuries BC The overthrow of the monarchy in 509 BC establishes the Roman Republic.

264 and 146 BC Rome defeats Carthage in the Punic Wars.

1st century BC–5th century AD Roman Empire. At its peak, it included all of the Mediterranean region and some regions beyond.

4th–6th centuries AD Christianity spreads under Constantine I.

AD 632 Muhammad's death starts the Arab, or Islamic, Empire, with more or less successive caliphates until the 13th century. At its peak it controlled three-quarters of the Mediterranean region.

12th century A revitalised Europe forms more organised and centralised states, and opposes expanding Muslim power. Though the Crusades fail to retake the Holy Land, they weaken the Byzantine Empire (the Greek-speaking Roman Empire centred on Constantinople), to the advantage of the Ottoman Turks.

14th–17th centuries The cultural movement known as the Renaissance begins in Italy and spreads around Europe.

1453	The fall of Constantine XI marks the end of the Byzantine Empire, and the Ottomans extend their reach from Greece and the Balkans to North Africa.
1571	The Battle of Lepanto sees the Holy League, a coalition of Catholic seafaring states orchestrated by Pope Pius, ending the Ottoman Turks' control of the eastern Mediterranean. The Turks and Spanish effectively split control of the region along geographical lines until the 18th century. Muslim rule is established along the North African coast.
18th century	The rise of Atlantic shipping allows naval trade to bypass the Mediterranean, in favour of Western Europe's Atlantic ports, and Northern Europe eclipses the region's former power hubs. The Ottoman Empire goes into decline.
19th century	European countries start to colonise North Africa, with Algeria and Tunisia, Egypt and Libya going

to France, Britain and Italy respectively.

1872–3	Thomas Cook organises the first round-the-world cruise through the Mediterranean.
1914–18	World War I sees the end of the Ottoman Empire, with Britain and France seizing its land.
1922	The independent state of Turkey is established.
1939–45	The region is beset by fighting as World War II rages.
1957	The European Economic Community, forerunner of the European Union, is established, by nations including France and Italy.
1980s	Greece, Spain and Portugal join the EU.
2008	A 43-member-state Union for the Mediterranean is launched to tackle issues such as the Middle East, immigration and pollution.
2009–10	Croatia's projected EU accession.
2013	Earliest possible date for Turkey's EU accession.

Culture

World culture owes a huge debt to the countries of the Mediterranean region. The area includes such diverse lands that the concept of a unified 'Mediterranean culture' as such is a fallacy. However, the heritage and exchange of the countries bordering the sea has sent cultural reverberations around the globe, in a vast range of disciplines from ancient architecture to contemporary film festivals.

Art

The history of art has its origins in the Mediterranean region, with the artistic traditions of Ancient Egypt, Ancient Greece and Rome all playing a formative role in the modern Western discipline. The success of such empires left an indelible imprint on the tenets of art, visible in, for example, the Greeks' use of the human body as a subject, and subsequent concentration on poise, proportion and anatomy. Early examples from the region are embodied by Ancient Egyptian art, which developed in the lower Nile Valley between around 5000 BC and around 300 BC. Excavated tombs and other archaeological sites yielded many works, marked by their simple figures in profile, adherence to rules and order and emphasis on the religious and social hierarchy (a pharaoh, for instance, would be depicted as larger than his underlings, regardless of whether this was physically the case).

The Romans took their cue from classical Greek art, and the cultural rebirth termed the Renaissance, which started in Italy, gave the art world titans such as Leonardo, Michelangelo and Raphael. Their work would be repeatedly imitated. The realistic linear perspective and naturalism of the Renaissance canon contrasted starkly with the simple forms of its Egyptian predecessor. But one similarity was the presence of religion: Christianity suffused the development of European art, particularly during the Middle Ages, although its influence has waned in the past two centuries. Politics is another common motif. Modernism, some of whose roots are in France (the impressionism of Monet and Manet), and its successor, postmodernism, grew up amid the disillusionment that followed World War II in Western Europe, fracturing the rigid rules of the previous schools. Today's Mediterranean region yields a diverse range of art.

Theatre

Much like art, Western theatre has its origins in the Mediterranean area. The first recorded staged drama dates back to 2000 BC, with the passion plays of Ancient Egypt, which focused on Osiris, the god of life, death and fertility. Formalisation of the theatrical tradition took place in Ancient Greece, where the concepts of tragedy and comedy, among other genres, were defined. Greek mythology featured heavily in plays from the period. The oldest surviving plays date from this era, and it was then that theatrical adjuncts such as criticism, architecture and acting as a profession took root.

Roman theatre borrowed significantly from Greece, with many plays of the epoch adapted from Greek ones. While religion was reduced in prominence, aesthetics increased, and war was depicted rather than just discussed. Raucous audiences meant plays often had to take the form of mimes, and relied on repetition and symbolic props and costumes. Later on, female actors (slaves) began to perform. Spain, Italy and France were among the Mediterranean countries that developed distinctive theatrical traditions throughout the Middle Ages, with genres including morality plays, mystery plays and *commedia dell'arte*, Italian improvisational theatre. Women's contribution, in particular, advanced in Spain during its Golden Age, from 1550 to 1700, despite the Catholic Church's opposition to their

The 16th-century *Rape of the Sabine Women* by Giambologna, in Florence, depicts a scene from early Roman history

participation and the theatre in general. In the middle of the 18th century, neoclassicism revived the theatrical (and other) traditions of Ancient Greece and Rome. Twentieth-century theatrical trends in the region included naturalism, realism, surrealism, absurdism and postmodernism.

Cinema

While it was Greece that gave cinema its name, from the Greek word for motion, the Mediterranean cannot claim to have played as great a role in its early development as the US. However, important film schools – Italian neorealism, French New Wave – have emerged from the region, and

European cinema has established itself as a more liberal, sometimes more experimental alternative to Hollywood. Several major festivals of the film world are also held in the Mediterranean – Cannes, the most high profile, as well as Venice (scene of the world's first major film festival in 1932), Rome, Thessaloniki, Istanbul, Marrakech, Cairo and Carthage.

Architecture

A quite staggering array of architectural gems is to be found in the region. Egypt's pyramids are one of the world's great wonders, and the country's legacy of cities, canals, dams and sphinxes are similarly splendid.

Civic ideals inspired Greek and Roman architecture, and the classical architecture that originated in Greece spread through much of Europe. The Renaissance shifted the spotlight onto the individual, allowing figures such as Michelangelo to become established names. Art Nouveau, which flourished at the turn of the 20th century, has also had a lasting effect on the region. It's perhaps most gloriously visible in Barcelona, in the works of Catalan architect Antonio Gaudí. In North Africa, Islamic architecture predominates, and mosques are a distinctive feature around the Mediterranean, from Marrakech to Istanbul.

The Theatre of Dionysus, cut into the Acropolis in Athens, was the first stone theatre ever built and seated around 17,000 people

Typical church architecture on the Greek islands, here at Mykonos

Literature

Perhaps the most famous symbol of Mediterranean literature is the library at Alexandria, which before its destruction was the largest library in the world. Greek poet Homer is probably the main early literary figure from the region, with the epic poems the *Iliad* and *Odyssey* still key texts, despite uncertainty over their writer's true identity and his precise dates. Literature progressed from its Ancient Egyptian and Greek origins into the Latin language, with Ovid and Virgil adapting Greek genres. Like art, much medieval literature was concerned with religion, with hagiographies and Florentine poet Dante's *Divina Commedia* being prime examples.

The advent of the printing press around 1439 revolutionised European literature, which thrived with the Renaissance's veneration of learning. Petrarch, Giovanni Boccaccio, Michel de Montaigne and François Rabelais shaped literature during the period, and France and Italy continued to spawn some of the most important world writers.

Music

Classical Greek traditions and the Catholic Church were two major influences on early music in the region. Musical styles associated with the area often betray the typically Mediterranean cultural mix: Spain's flamenco, for example, has Islamic influences, while Algerian folk music *raï* mixes Bedouin sounds with Spanish, French, African and Arabic styles.

Folklore and mythology

The rich vein of mythology from Greece, which was developed by Rome, is explored in more detail on pp90–91.

Festivals and events

Around the Mediterranean, many festivals, events and public holidays have a religious origin, Christian to the north, Muslim to the south. But there is plenty of secular fun to be had too, with a clutch of esteemed film festivals, and an abundance of events celebrating drama, music and food, with processions and the like. With so much territory covered, it's impossible to list them all, but the following should give a flavour.

FRANCE
Cannes
Le Festival de Cannes
(Cannes Film Festival)
Glitzy and glamorous (even the much-besmirched paparazzi come in tuxedos), Cannes is one of the world's most prestigious film festivals. Consisting of various competitive and non-competitive sections, a film that does well here (for example, by winning the top prize, the Palme d'Or) generally has it made. (For more on Cannes, *see pp54–5.*)
Usually May.
Palais des Festivals et des Congrès.
www.festival-cannes.fr

ITALY
Rome
Festa de Noantri (Festival of We Others)
The 16th-century group of fishermen who purportedly caught a statue of the Madonna in their nets are the premise for the Festa de Noantri. Though the crux of the event remains the procession of the statue through the streets, things have more of a neighbourhood rather than a religious feel, with street theatre, dancing, music and a market.
Eight days in mid-July.
www.romaturismo.com

Venice
Festa del Redentore
(Festival of the Redeemer)
Around two thousand boats come to view the spectacular hour-long firework display, the high point of this two-day event. Festa del Redentore is held to celebrate the end of a plague in 1575–7, which killed a third of the inhabitants of Venice, including the Renaissance painter Titian.
Third Saturday and Sunday of July.
www.comune.venezia.it

SPAIN
Barcelona
Festes de la Mercè
(Festival of Our Lady of Mercy)
The city's main festival includes competitions to see who can build the

Fireworks light up the old city of Dubrovnik at the start of the Summer Festival

highest human tower, processions, live music, papier-mâché figures and fire-breathing 'dragons', all washed down with plenty of cava.
Week of 24 September.
www.bcn.cat

CROATIA
Dubrovnik
Dubrovačke Ljetne Igre
(Dubrovnik Summer Festival)
Lasting for around six weeks, Dubrovnik's annual do consists of classical music, theatre, opera and dance at over 70 outdoor venues. Local works and performers feature heavily, but there's also the odd Shakespeare play and foreign musician.
July and August.
www.dubrovnik-festival.hr

GREECE
Athens
Athens Epidaurus Festival
Dating back over half a century, the festival's remit is to bridge the gap between Greece's artistic traditions and a more experimental take on the arts. Music, theatre, dance and visual arts all feature, at a variety of venues, both classical and contemporary.
June and July.
www.greekfestival.gr

TURKEY
Ramazan
Muslims (which theoretically includes almost all Turks) are expected to desist from eating, drinking, sex and smoking (no small task, given the nation's devotion to nicotine) during daylight hours. While all this might not sound like much fun, the abstainers make up for it after dark with ceremonial feasting, drumming (to wake worshippers for their pre-dawn meal) and a generally carnival atmosphere. Ramazan, or Ramadan, is observed in other Muslim countries too.
Varies with the lunar calendar.

TUNISIA
Tunis
Mediterranean Guitar Festival
World-famous guitarists take their place alongside local practitioners during this five-day music extravaganza. Events are staged at locations throughout Tunis.
March.
www.festmedguitar.com

Highlights

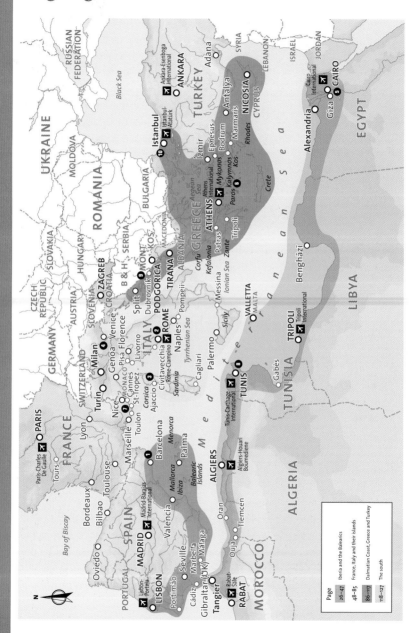

Page	
26–47	Iberia and the Balearics
48–85	France, Italy and their islands
86–117	Dalmatian Coast, Greece and Turkey
118–127	The south

❶ Architecture of Barcelona It may be the jaw-dropping Art Nouveau creations of Catalan architect Gaudí – such as La Sagrada Família – that win the plaudits, but even the blocks of flats in Barcelona are appealing (*see pp37–41*).

❷ Rome Containing an entire separate state in the form of the Vatican City, plus a wealth of other renowned attractions, Rome well deserves its moniker, *Caput Mundi*, Capital of the World (*see pp70–73*).

❸ Beaches of Corsica There is no shortage of great stretches of shore on the Mediterranean coastline, but Corsica's fabulous beaches get top marks even by the high standards of the Med (*see pp59–60*).

❹ Venice It has been pronounced the most beautiful city in the world, and walking around the unique 'City of Water', you'll be unlikely to disagree (*see pp82–5*).

❺ Excursion to Egyptian pyramids The only one of the Seven Wonders of the Ancient World still in existence is well worth the dusty desert trek (*see pp119 & 122*).

❻ The Cyclades Cobbled alleyways and whitewashed houses, punctuated by the occasional brilliant cascade of flowers, the impossibly picturesque Cyclades are the quintessence of the Greek islands (*see pp101–3*).

❼ Glamour of St-Tropez Celeb-spotters should head for St-Tropez, the resort *du jour* of A-listers from P. Diddy to Paris Hilton (*see pp51–2*).

❽ Markets in Tunis Have your haggling skills at the ready in the colourful souks of Tunis (*see pp125–6*).

❾ Dubrovnik There's plenty to see in this beautiful Croatian port, not least the UNESCO World Heritage Site of the old city (*see pp88–9*).

❿ Istanbul Bridging Europe and Asia, Istanbul is an absorbing melange of east and west, with a plethora of cultural highlights thrown in for good measure (*see pp104–6*).

There are fascinating shops in the souks of Tunis

Cruising routes

Logistics obviously make it difficult to abandon a cruise midway through, so it's essential you choose the right one in the first place. Aside from the level of luxury you require, it's important also to consider the emphasis – while some cruises are about daytime sightseeing, gentle leisure activities like quoits and bingo and an early night, others offer partying until sunrise. Price, duration and destination are other crucial considerations.

Basic research can ensure that you won't end up on the wrong kind of holiday. Cruise company websites usually give some idea of what kind of passenger they are suited to. Check holiday review websites for the input of previous passengers. Sites geared specifically towards cruise holidays include *www.cruisecritic.co.uk*, *www.cruisemates.com*, *www.reviewthatcruise.com* and *www.ship-happens.co.uk*. Reviews can also be found on general travel sites, such as *www.reviewcentre.com*. There are also hefty tomes on the subject, such as the *Berlitz Complete Guide to Cruising and Cruise Ships*, or Fodor's *The Complete Guide to European Cruises*, which list several hundred options and include full ship details plus advice on the level of formality, and other aspects that might affect your choice. (They even offer a breakdown of how much to tip on each cruise liner.)

Differences are manifold. Party animals will probably want a ship that stays in each port overnight, or at least late enough for the place's nightlife to be adequately sampled, plus an on-board disco. Sightseers, on the other hand, are likely to be happier with an itinerary that includes early arrivals, evening departures and nights spent at sea. Some ships are suited to families, others to couples, some to the young and others to the older. Facilities that may, or may not, be crucial to your enjoyment include a spa, gym, shop, entertainment or a particular dining experience (homely cuisine or something more upmarket and adventurous). Entertainment to you might be casino games and pub quizzes, or yoga and alternative comedy. All of this should be covered in the sources cited above. Specialist tours (as diverse as a Christian tour of the lands of the Bible and a ballroom dancing cruise) can also be found.

The distinctions of price, duration and destination are easier to factor in. Long gone are the days when cruising was the preserve of the rich. The cheapest sea-bound holidays are probably the easyCruise (a no-frills model from the easyJet company), or a last-minute, out-of-season deal on one of the mid-range options – usually for one week only and in an inside cabin. Either of these can be had for as little as £300 per person, including meals. At the

The lobby of an Ocean Village cruise ship

other end of the scale, a two-week trip staying in a cabin with a balcony could set you back ten times as much, without even entering the luxury market. The rule that you get what you pay for generally applies in the cruising world although, if you are flexible, can go outside of peak season and are prepared to book at the last minute, there are some excellent bargains to be had.

When doing your research, don't make the mistake of just giving the price a cursory glance; instead check precisely what is included. While most totals would be inclusive of meals, for example, some may not. Hidden extras can push up the cost of your holiday considerably. If you're on a tight budget, even a detail as small as whether water is provided free with your meal, or you have to buy bottled, can be significant. As a rule, the more expensive ships tend to charge for fewer extras, while booking a lower-cost trip might well result in your having to pay more charges once on board.

Duration is usually a simple choice between one week and two, although you sometimes find eight-, ten- or twelve-day holidays, and there are also long-weekend options available. A few ships sail for up to a month. Obviously, how long you choose to sail for depends on your schedule, but bear in mind that most week-long cruises cover less distance (this sounds obvious, but is not always the case – some two-week cruises retrace the same route in the second week, with just minor differences in which ports are visited).

Passengers walking by their grand floating hotel near Mykonos Town

your journey in the UK, you may also stop in Portugal, en route to the Med itself. Eastern cruises typically depart from Venice, Istanbul or Athens, and sail to Turkey and the Greek islands, sometimes with a stop on the Dalmatian Coast. Some itineraries take in a North African or non-EU island destination (a stop outside the European Union allows the ship to conduct duty-free sales). A few itineraries focus on the eastern reaches, including Egypt.

DIY cruises

Travellers who like the idea of a holiday at sea without the captive element of a cruise might consider a DIY journey – getting around the region by ferry. Logistically, this would be relatively easy to do. The Med has an extensive ferry network, and many of the legs done by cruise could be completed by domestic and international services. However, the economies of scale offered by the package deal of a cruise mean that financial savings with a DIY cruise are highly unlikely. Add to that the hassle of dealing with different vessels, and frequent packing and unpacking, means that there is probably little to be gained from going it alone, particularly if you're going for a short time. Where a DIY cruise would make sense would be as part of a longer trip, where you intended to spend several days in each port. In this case, the ferry would make a hassle-free alternative to a driving holiday, or a good way to get your car across the water.

As with other holidays, it's not usually the case that a two-week cruise will cost double the price of a one-week one – going for two weeks often means you pay a substantially lower rate per day.

While price and duration will matter, of more importance to many travellers will be the ports you are able to visit. This is contingent on the length of the cruise and the size of the ship. For convenience, many routes are circular, but one-way cruises, which allow you to travel further from your starting point, are sometimes available.

Operators usually divide the Mediterranean up into west and east. Western itineraries, often the more popular, will probably stop at the 'big three' – Spain, France and Italy – normally starting in Spain. If you begin

A local ferry in Turkey

Iberia and the Balearics

Lying at the southwestern outreaches of Europe, the Iberian Peninsula's weather and geography has long made it a destination of choice for holidaymakers from Europe's northern, cooler climes. Traditional seafaring nations, Spain and Portugal (a Mediterranean country in spirit if not in actuality) have been enriched by contributions from a range of countries, one of the factors behind their vibrancy. Another is the easy living best encapsulated in the siesta, or afternoon nap.

Though it is a package-tourist magnet, there is far more to the peninsula than sun, sea, sand and sangria – though of course you can find those in abundance too. As Catholic countries, Spain and Portugal have a legacy of glorious cathedrals. Family values and a laidback pace of life make their stunning coasts the ideal holiday venue, and tourism has established itself as the main economic driver of the region. Consequently, hospitality is all-pervasive.

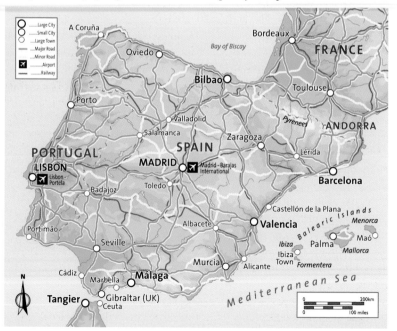

The River Tagus from a steep street in Lisbon

Though they are often lumped together (they are in fact a province, or autonomous community), the Balearic Islands, an archipelago off the eastern coast of the peninsula, are geographically and culturally diverse. Palma, the capital city of the province, shares much with mainland Spain, its awe-inspiring cathedral showcasing Catholic supremacy. But piety is not on the menu in Ibiza, the Med's capital of hedonism.

But whether you go for the beaches, the bars or the biblical, Iberia and its islands are popular cruise stops. Even if you stay just a day, the rich, flavoursome food, flashes of colour and culture and extraordinarily pretty beaches (among Europe's best) will leave a brilliant impression.

PORTUGAL
Lisbon

Travellers sailing into Lisbon are greeted by the 16th-century Gothic-style Belém Tower, built to commemorate Portugal's great seafaring son Vasco da Gama. Ships dock at one of the quays on the River Tagus, from where buses 28, 201, 714, 727, 729, 751 and tram 15 go to the city centre. Smaller ships sometimes dock at Santa Apolónia, from where you can walk.

Though the bustle of Lisbon confirms its de facto status as a capital city, its terracotta roofs, cobblestone streets, wrought-iron balconies and lack of skyscrapers give the city a more laidback feel than most modern metropolises. Built on seven hills, the multicultural influences that have shaped Europe's westernmost capital are evident in the odd Arabic place name, not to mention the cuisine. But the predominant aesthetic in the architecture is Catholicism, with several churches and monasteries among the city's main sights. Part of the pleasure of a visit to Lisbon is simply wandering, along the alleyways, around the *praças* (squares), and down the pedestrianised shopping streets.

Alfama

Unlike its neighbouring district of Baixa, which is characterised by neat geometrical lines, Alfama is a warren of alleyways. When the Moors dominated the region in the 8th century, this district and the city were effectively one and the same. Subsequently populated by Lisbon's poor, its fishing community and African immigrants, labyrinthine Alfama has retained its edginess and exoticism – which has in later years attracted *fado*-playing restaurants and tourist shops in droves. A rare survivor of the devastating earthquake of the 18th century, the neighbourhood conceals all manner of pretty buildings, and its steep streets afford good views. *East of Baixa.*

Castelo de São Jorge (St George's Castle)

Occupying the city's highest hill, Lisbon's flagship fortress was a pivotal site in the ongoing battles between the Moors and Christians. The building,

much changed over the nearly two millennia since its foundation, has at times housed a barracks, prison, royal residence, theatre and charity. From the 1940s, many of the ill-fitting additions have been removed, and the site is now one of the city's top tourist draws, not least for the fine views it affords.

Overlooking the Alfama. Open: Nov–Feb daily 9am–6pm; Mar–Oct daily 9am–9pm. Admission charge. Bus: 37; tram: 28.

Sé de Lisboa (Lisbon Cathedral)

The city's oldest church dates from the 12th century, and additions and amendments over the subsequent centuries have led to a mix of

A tram runs along a street in the Baixa district of Lisbon

FADO

Portugal's best-known style of music derives its name from the word for 'fate'. Its mournful songs often broached topics such as life at sea, or the privations of poverty, and many conveyed the feeling of pining for someone or something. Although reckoned to have begun in the 1820s, many believe it originated much earlier, a fusion of local sailor songs with African slave rhythms and Arabic traditions. Though tainted by its association with fascism (it was said to be one of the three Fs – along with football and the holy town of Fátima – that underpinned Antonio Salazar's regime), *fado*'s popularity survived, and since its most famous exponent – Amália Rodrigues – died in 1999, a new generation of singers has emerged to take up the mantle.

architectural styles, from Romanesque via Gothic to Baroque. Visitors might like to see the relics of Vincent of Saragossa, the city's patron saint. A highlight is the impressive rose window. *Largo de Sé. Tel: (218) 876 628, (218) 866 752. Open: Tue–Sat 9am–7pm, Sun & Mon 9am–5pm. Free admission. Bus: 37; tram: 12, 28.*

Baixa

Built to a grid system after the 1755 earthquake that razed much of the city to the ground, Lisbon's downtown area is a candidate for UNESCO World Heritage Site status. The city's retail and banking district exudes neat, neoclassical charm, with Art Deco storefronts, pavement mosaics and proud columns and statues. Baixa takes its full name, Baixa Pombalina, from the Marquis of Pombal, who led the

city's post-earthquake reconstruction, and the architectural measures he took to guard against a repeat of the seismic damage remain an early example of canny urban planning. 'Elegant' is the adjective most commonly used to describe the zone, and it's certainly apt. The grace of the buildings is offset by activity: street performers and vendors, tramcars, and Portuguese people relaxing over a drink in one of the many cafés.
Between the Cais do Sodré railway station and the Alfama.

Portimão

The approach to Portimão passes Algarvian cliff faces and rock formations, plus the hotels that dot the coast. Since dredging works were completed in 2008, all but the largest vessels can now dock at the port, in the river mouth, replacing the previous tender system. Cruise companies usually lay on buses to take visitors the few miles to the town centre and the beach.

Portimão may not boast the clutch of high-profile attractions of some other ports on and around the Iberian Peninsula, but it's more than just a gateway to the Algarve, Portugal's fertile holiday region. The town's status as a busy fishing port gives it an authenticity missing in some of the more touristy stops in the region. A medieval city, Portimão's old centre is made up of two-storey buildings adorned by typically Mediterranean wrought-iron balconies and *azulejos*,

The seafront at Portimão

the colourful ceramic tiles that help give Portuguese towns their lustre. One of the pleasures of stopping off here is just strolling through the old town.

Another is hitting the beach. Portimão is blessed with a surfeit of fine stretches of sand on which to do some sun-soaking. (Good weather is in plentiful supply here, with the local tourist authorities promising around 300 days of sunshine a year.) Whether you're happy to set down your towel next to the legions of holidaymakers on long Alvor beach, or prefer the privacy of Três Irmãos and Prainha, small segments of sand separated by rocky ochre outcrops, beach lovers will be spoilt for choice.

Lacking the must-see places of other cruise ports, Portimão presents an ideal opportunity for shopping. The main two shopping streets are Rua Comercial (as the name suggests) and Rua Vasco da Gama, where you can pick up locally made clothes and souvenirs. Fresh produce is on sale until 2pm from Monday to Saturday at the town market. And keen shoppers who happen to pitch up on the first Monday of the month can rummage around at the large travelling market hosted at the Parque de Feiras e Exposições de Portimão.

182km (113 miles) south of Lisbon.

SPAIN
Cádiz

The approach to Cádiz has little in the way of sights aside from the city itself. Cruise ships dock at the port's Alfonso VIII quay. From there, it's a ten-minute walk to the action. After you disembark, turn left and head for the port gate, which is opposite a useful information kiosk.

Capital of the Andalucian province of the same name, the university town of Cádiz is reputed to be the oldest continuously inhabited city in Western Europe. It's a small and easily navigable place, marked by Moorish houses, pretty balconies and narrow, twisting alleyways. In the tourism stakes, it is largely overshadowed by its neighbour Seville, to which it bears some resemblance. Cádiz has a typically Spanish selection of highlights, the flagship one being the **Catedral de Cádiz**. This impressive structure is predominantly Baroque in style, with elements of the rococo and neoclassical, thanks to its protracted construction period and several changes of architect. It's also known as Catedral Nueva or the New Cathedral – something of a misnomer now as it dates from the 18th century. Climbing the stairs, though tiring, affords excellent views. *Behind Plaza de San Juan de Dios. www.torredeponiente.com. Open: 15 Jun–15 Sept daily 10am–8pm; 16 Sept–14 Jun daily 10am–6pm. Admission charge.*

Iberia and the Balearics

Plaza de San Juan de Dios in the old town of Cádiz

More information about the area can be gleaned at the **Museo Provincial**. Starting from Phoenician and Roman times, the museum charts the history of the area through art and artefacts. Exhibits include works by Rubens and Tía Norica puppets.

Plaza de Mina. Tel: (956) 203 368. Open: Tue 2.30–8.30pm, Wed–Sat 9am–8.30pm, Sun & public holidays 9am–2.30pm. Closed: Mon. Free admission with proof of EU citizenship.

290km (180 miles) southeast of Portimão.

La Giralda and the Catedral de Santa María in Seville

Seville

The limitations of Seville's cruise port mean that only the smallest ships can travel along the River Guadalquivir to dock in town. It is most often seen on a day trip from Cádiz. If you're not on an organised tour, the best way to visit is by train. Journey times start at around an hour and a half.

Andalucía's capital serves as a vibrant microcosm of Spain. Its diverse cultural legacy (the town's 2,000-year history takes in the Romans, Vandals, Visigoths and Moors before the Christians got control of it) has manifested itself in its patchwork architecture. Formerly one of the richest ports in Europe, Seville's Renaissance and Baroque buildings betray the grandeur of their heritage. Chief among them is the **Catedral de Santa María de la Sede**, a UNESCO World Heritage Site and the fourth largest Christian church in the world. Also the world's largest Gothic cathedral, it somewhat incongruously adjoins a minaret, **La Giralda**, which was part of the 12th-century mosque the church replaced.
Catedral de Santa María de la Sede, Calle Alemanes. No tel. Open: Mon–Sat 11am–5pm, Sun 2.30–6pm. Admission charge except on Sun.

With a religious imprint of a different hue, the district of **Santa Cruz**, to the southeast of the city, is an erstwhile Jewish ghetto. Today it's a buzzing tourist zone, with quaint alleys emerging onto unexpected plazas, tapas bars and swish houses. The area is also home to the **Alcázares Reales de Sevilla**, or Royal Alcazars of Seville. The palace, built as a Muslim fortress, has housed both Islamic and Christian nobles, which is reflected in its diverse architecture.
Alcázares Reales de Sevilla. Open: Tue– Sat 9.30am–5pm, Sun & public holidays 9.30am–1.30pm. Admission charge.

100km (62 miles) northeast of Cádiz.

Gibraltar

The port is a 2km (1¼-mile) walk from the centre of Gibraltar along a straight road. If you don't fancy walking and no shuttle has been laid on, there should be an abundance of taxis (with meters) awaiting passengers.

A little – and fiercely disputed – piece of Britain on the end of the Iberian Peninsula, Gibraltar is something of a geographical and political quirk. The territory, which essentially consists of a protuberance of limestone, occupied a vital strategic position, and was repeatedly fought over by adversaries of the time. For the last three centuries, it has been a British colony – despite Spanish attempts to wrest it back. Gibraltar is a slightly surreal combination of the UK and Spain, with which it has a border. British clichés and symbols such as double-decker buses, pubs and pints, fish and chips, the pound and the British bobby (policeman) are all to be found, bathed in Mediterranean sunshine.

The unmistakeable Rock of Gibraltar

Given the colony's convoluted history, it's worth making at stop at the **Gibraltar Museum**, which attempts to explain it. As well as a 15-minute film, there are various galleries containing archaeological finds, old photographs and a detailed scale model of the Rock, among other exhibits.

THE ROCK OF GIBRALTAR

The limestone promontory at Europe's southwestern tip was one of the two Pillars of Hercules that flanked the Strait of Gibraltar, connecting the Atlantic Ocean to the Mediterranean Sea, and dividing Europe and Africa. In Greek mythology, Hercules is said to have formed the strait by crashing through the mountain. The Rock has proved similarly sturdy. Throughout lengthy sieges, its people did not capitulate, and the colony's motto, *Nulli Expugnabilis Hosti* (Latin for 'no enemy shall expel us'), encapsulates the local pride in this fortitude. The result is the idiom 'solid as the Rock of Gibraltar'.

18/20 Bomb House Lane.
Tel: 200 74289. Email: enquiries@ museum.gib.gi. www.gib.gi/museum. Open: Mon–Fri 10am–6pm, Sat 10am–2pm. Admission charge. Bus: 3.

95km (59 miles) southeast of Cádiz.

Málaga
Málaga's harbour is within walking distance of the city centre.

Chiefly famous as the gateway to the Costa del Sol, Málaga is also the birthplace of Pablo Picasso. Moorish influence is visible here, in buildings such as the **Alcazaba**. Dating from the 8th century, it also contains an archaeological museum. Right next to it is the **Teatro Romano** (Roman Amphitheatre). After centuries lying undiscovered, it is now used for drama, and has hosted performances from such luminaries as local lad Antonio Banderas.

Alcazaba. Calle Alcazabilla. Tel: (952) 216 005. Open: summer, Tue–Sun 9am–8pm; winter, Tue–Sun 9am–7pm. Closed: Mon. Free admission.

Teatro Romano. Calle Alcazabilla 2. Tel: (952) 128 830. Open: Nov–Mar Wed–Sat 10am–2.30pm & 4–7pm, Sun 10am–2.30pm; Apr–Oct Wed–Sat 10am–2.30pm & 5–8pm. Free admission.

Málaga's more famous son is commemorated in the **Museo Picasso Málaga** (Picasso Museum). Described by Picasso's descendants as the fulfilment of the artist's lifelong dream, the collection includes works donated by the family. Exhibits trace the Andalucian's work from his juvenilia to his more mature creations.

Museo Picasso Málaga. Palacio de Buenavista, Calle San Agustín. Tel: (952) 127 600. Email: info@museopicassomalaga.org.

www.museopicassomalaga.org. Open: Tue–Thur, Sun & public holidays 10am–8pm, Fri & Sat 10am–9pm. Closed: Mon. Admission charge.

106km (66 miles) northeast of Gibraltar.

Marbella

Marbella is most often seen on an excursion from Málaga, from where regular buses make the approximately 45-minute journey.

A chance car problem lies behind the flashy image that has come to characterise the Costa del Sol resort of Marbella (pronounced Mar-bay-ah). When a Rolls-Royce belonging to German aristocrats Prince Max Egon zu Hohenlohe-Langenburg and Alfonso de Hohenlohe needed attention in the vicinity, Marbella was a fishing village with fewer than 1,000 inhabitants. Struck by the area's potential, Alfonso began buying land in 1947, and the town became known as a fashionable holiday destination for the glitterati, with royals, business moguls and Hollywood stars holidaying there. The glamour is embodied in the Golden Mile, a strip of upmarket clubs, hotels, eateries and yachts that runs from Marbella to Puerto Banus. The resort has continued to play host to the rich and famous, including, rather improbably, a then-unknown Osama bin Laden.

Although the Russian Mafia brought a seamy side to Marbella, and

The Moorish Alcazaba in Málaga

inappropriate building work has tarnished the port's charm a little, it retains its reputation as a playground for the rich. It has the usual Spanish selection of sights. The **Museo del Grabado Español Contemporáneo de Marbella** (Marbella Modern Art Museum) contains works by some of Spain's best-known artists. More quirkily, there is also a **Museo del Bonsai** (Bonsai Museum).

Museo del Grabado Español Contemporáneo de Marbella. Calle Hospital Bazán. Tel: (952) 765 741. Email: info@museodelgrabado.com. www.museodelgrabado.com. Open: Mon & Sat 9am–2pm, Tue–Fri 9am–2pm & 6–9pm. Closed: Sun & public holidays. Admission charge.

Museo del Bonsai. Parque Arroyo de la Represa. Tel: (952) 862 926. Open: daily 10am–1.30pm & 4.30–8pm. Admission charge.

The chief pleasure of Marbella, though, is simply strolling past the exclusive haunts, and through the old town around Plaza de los Naranjos. People-watching from a pavement café is another amusing pastime, and you may even spot one of the current crop of celebrity Marbella fans, said to include Antonio Banderas and Melanie Griffiths, Bruce Willis, Paul McCartney and David Beckham. Be warned: local cafés are not cheap.

47km (29 miles) southwest of Málaga.

Valencia

Valencia's port is an enjoyable but longish – 4km (2½-mile) – walk from the city centre. If your cruise line does not lay on a shuttle service between the port and the Plaza del Ayuntamiento, take bus 19. A taxi will make the journey for a reasonable sum.

A quiet street in Marbella's old town

The spectacular Ciudad de las Artes y las Ciencias in Valencia was designed by locally born architect Santiago Calatrava

Vibrant Valencia, Spain's third biggest city, has the usual complement of highlights: an old district with coiling alleyways and edifices dating back to Roman and Arabic eras, a lively nightlife, a clutch of pretty plazas and a Gothic cathedral. The city is easily navigable on foot, with the majority of sights on or around the Plaza del Ayuntamiento. Like many other Spanish city cathedrals, Valencia's blends elements of the Romanesque, Gothic and Baroque. What distinguishes it, however, is its claim to contain the Holy Grail, the cup Jesus is said to have used at the Last Supper. The adjoining tower, the **Miguelete**, was part of the old mosque that occupied the site. The climb up the tower is repaid with superb views.
Plaza de la Reina. Tel: (963) 918 127. Open Mon–Sat 7.30am–1pm & 4.30–8.30pm, Sun 7.30am–1pm & 5–8.30pm. Admission charge.

For a more modern outing, try the **Ciudad de las Artes y las Ciencias** (City of Arts and Sciences). This huge complex consists of an arts palace where opera, dance and theatre are staged, a garden, an IMAX cinema, science museum and aquarium. The attraction could easily absorb a whole day, or longer.
Avenida Autopista del Saler. Tel: (902) 100 031; www.cac.es. Open: low season, daily approximately 10am–7pm, high season, daily 10am–9pm; opening hours of the separate sections vary – consult the website for details. Admission charge.

468km (291 miles) northeast of Málaga.

Barcelona
Barcelona is heralded by Montjuïc, or the Hill of the Jews, after which you'll soon spot the marina. Cruise liners dock to the south of the city. Because of the size of the terminal, it may take as little as ten minutes to walk to the south end of La Rambla, the road leading into the heart of the city; however, if your ship is berthed at the other end, it will take

much longer. Shuttles run every 20 minutes, and there will also be plenty of taxis at the port.

One of Europe and the Mediterranean's most engaging cities, the Catalonian capital is teeming with delights, architectural, cultural and gastronomic. As you wander round the centre, it seems there is scarcely a street that doesn't have a point of interest; indeed, Barcelona's 'normal' buildings are often more impressive than other cities' trumpeted attractions. An army of vivid performing artists complement the astonishing architecture, all of which is offset by the dazzling blue of the Med in the background. After the sun goes down there are myriad venues for partying, or you can simply enjoy

Detail of the Passion façade on Gaudí's church of La Sagrada Família in Barcelona

the tapas on a restaurant terrace and watch the street musicians and performers ply their trades.

Barri Gòtic (Gothic Quarter)
Delineated by ancient Roman walls, some of which are still visible, the Barri Gòtic (Gothic quarter), provides some of Barcelona's best wandering territory. Narrow passageways open onto stylish squares, with space limitations keeping motorised traffic to a minimum. Inviting boutiques, medieval buildings and buskers all contribute to the special atmosphere. While random wandering will be handsomely rewarded, it is worth seeking out **La Seu**. Construction of the cathedral – extraordinarily striking, even by Spain's high standards – began in the 13th century, though the Gothic façade is a 19th-century addition. The cloister is home to 13 white geese – which compete admirably with the impressive construction for tourist attention – commemorating the age of Saint Eulalia of Barcelona when she is said to have been martyred. *Plaça de la Seu. www.catedralbcn.org. Open: Mon–Fri 8am–1.30pm & 4–7.30pm, Sat & Sun 8am–1.30pm & 5–7.30pm. Admission charge for certain sections.*

Gaudí architecture
If one individual can be said to have changed the face of Barcelona, it must be modernist architect Antonio Gaudí. His Art Nouveau creations are extraordinarily beautiful, eclipsing even

the city's other superlative attractions with their ambition and flamboyance. The flagship Gaudí structure is **La Sagrada Família**. Work started in 1882 and has yet to be completed, but its unfinished state does not detract from the soaring towers and vivid detail of this Roman Catholic church (not even a cathedral). If your time is limited to one site in Barcelona, this should be it.

Plaça de la Sagrada Família, corner of Carrers de Sardenya & de Majorca. No tel. www.sagradafamilia.cat. Open: Apr–Sept 9am–8pm; Oct–Mar 9am–6pm. Admission charge.

Park Güell, Gaudí's awe-inspiring move into landscape gardening, is also home to **Casa Museu Gaudí** (Gaudí House Museum). The architect's former home now houses a collection of his designs and busts, as well as some furniture.

Park Güell. Carrer Nou de Las Ramblas. Open: winter 10am–7pm; summer 10am–9pm. Free admission. Casa Museu Gaudí. Tel: (93) 219 3811. Open: Oct–Mar 10am–6pm; Apr–Sept 10am–8pm. Admission charge.

La Rambla

By day teeming with flower stalls, performance artists and tourists, and by night dotted with con artists, prostitutes and illicit beer sellers, this leafy, pedestrianised street is the heart of the city. Whatever the time is, there is always activity. Chief among the attractions are the legion of human

Cafés shaded by trees make La Rambla a pleasant street to pass the time in

statues and street artists, from the talented (fire jugglers and football whizzes) to the comical (concealed artists jumping out of their box to shock inattentive tourists) to the bizarre (the woman covered in fruit). Night brings out the seamier side of the city, which is still fascinating to observe. Avoid, at all costs, the matchbox scam, where gullible tourists are tricked into betting which matchbox a ball is under. Previous 'winners' are always part of the gang; once you bet, the ball will be spirited away by sleight of hand, as will your money. La Rambla is lined with cafés and newsstands, and is a wonderful place to sit and people-watch – although expect to pay heavily for the privilege.

301km (187 miles) northeast of Valencia.

Walk: Barcelona

A walker's city through and through, Barcelona will repay almost any stroll you take in and around its centre. The following route focuses on a small area around La Rambla. With a museum, a market, a statue, a cathedral and some leisure factored in, it's an excellent microcosm of what the Catalonian capital has to offer.

This short walk can be done in two hours, at a push, but leave three if you want to savour the sights.

Start at Liceu metro station and turn north along La Rambla.

1 La Rambla

Barcelona's lively boulevard is described in more detail on p39.

Walk along La Rambla until you see the entrance to the market on the left.

2 La Boqueria

One of the city's most popular markets, La Boqueria, also known as

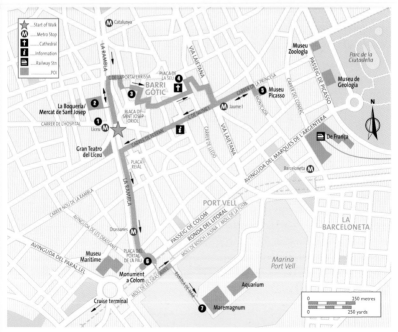

Mercat de Sant Josep (St Joseph's Market), is a colourful emporium selling fresh produce from fruit to fish, plus spices and sweets. Though much of the produce may be of limited interest to a tourist, you can pick up a fresh juice, or simply soak up the lively atmosphere.
Continue along La Rambla and go right almost immediately onto Carrer de la Portaferrissa. The streets on your right make up the Gothic Quarter.

3 Barri Gòtic (Gothic Quarter)

Described in more detail on p38, the Gothic Quarter is suited to pleasant meandering.
Your wandering should eventually bring you out at La Seu, just east of Carrer de la Portaferrissa.

4 La Seu

For more on Barcelona's impressive cathedral, *see p38.*
East of the cathedral, join Via Laietana and walk towards the sea. Turn left onto Carrer de la Princesa. After about 250m (275 yds), the Museu Picasso is off to your right.

5 Museu Picasso (Picasso Museum)

Over two thousand works donated by the artist himself make this one of Barcelona's top museums.
Montcada 15–23. Tel: (93) 256 3000. www.museupicasso.bcn.es. Open: Tue–Sun 8am–10pm. Closed: Mon. Admission charge. Go back along Carrer de la Princesa to La Rambla and turn left. You'll soon see the statue of Columbus.

6 Monument a Colom (Columbus Monument)

Taking the lift the 60m (200ft) to the top of the Columbus Monument provides a good view of the city and will help newcomers get their bearings. You can watch tourists posing with the lions at the base.
Portal de la Pau. Open: daily 9am–8.30pm. Admission charge. Cross the road here and continue towards the waterfront.

7 The waterfront

Barcelona's relaxing quay area has plenty of places to stop for a brief rest or bite to eat, to round off the walk.

The Monument a Colom stands near the port at the end of La Rambla

The Balearics

Often lumped together as a holiday destination, the 50 islands that make up this archipelago are in fact quite distinctive. The Balearics' geographical separateness from Spain is reflected in an island mentality: the Catalan-speaking islanders have a strong sense of their identity that has resisted the homogenising effects of tourism. Though what might spring to mind first are the wild nightclubs of Ibiza, the islands are also home to quiet fishing villages, mountains, cathedrals and ancient ruins.

Ibiza

The approach to Ibiza Town (also called Eivissa) affords pleasing views of the Dalt Villa, the old town surrounded by ramparts on the hilltop. Ships dock at the Passeig Marítim, from where the centre of town is easily reachable on foot.

The third largest of the Balearics, Ibiza is perhaps the best known for its unofficial status as the clubbing capital of Europe (for more details on its club scene, *see pp46–7*). But there is plenty more to the island than the frenzied hedonism for which it is famous. Today's nightlife developed from the hippy scene that reached its peak in the 1970s, a scene that still survives in small enclaves and in the popular markets and boutiques that attract the 'alternative' shopper.

After clubbing and soaking up the sun, shopping is perhaps the next most popular activity. Retail is designed with the trendy consumer in mind, and you can pick up everything from top of the range hi-fis to vintage clothing and a plethora of chic accessories. The best place for shopping is **Ibiza Town**, with the port area of Sa Penya brimming with boutiques and market stalls. If you

A typical countryside scene in Ibiza

The islands of Es Vedrà and Vedranell lie off the southwest coast of Ibiza

don't want to shop with the hoi polloi, San Carlos, north of Santa Eulària, hosts the Saturday **Hippy Market** on Santa Eulària road (*open: 10am–late*). On Wednesdays, **Es Canar**, in the northeast, becomes the market town (*open: Apr–Oct 10am–7pm*).

The standard image of Ibizan beaches as chock-full of bleary-eyed ravers sleeping off the excesses of the night before may have some truth on the tourist circuit, but the island also has some less discovered stretches of sand where a little more space can be found. Cala Boix, on the northeast coastline, has the distinction of being the only dark sand beach in all the Balearics. Its surrounding hills provide a degree of seclusion. Another quieter section of shoreline is the small Cala Salada, surrounded by pine-forested hills on the west side of the island. For a chic spot of sand, the beach at Ses Salines, in the south of the island, is a large expanse of beach adjoined by plenty of bars and restaurants. Also in the south, Es Cavallet, the official nudist beach, is popular with gay travellers. Southwest lies the popular and laidback Cala d'Hort, with its view of the island of Es Vedrà. The northern coast features sheltered Cala Xarraca near Portinatx, set in a large bay and popular with snorkellers, plus the relatively undeveloped Cala Benirràs, close to Port de Sant Miquel. In total, there are around 60 beaches on Ibiza, so you shouldn't find yourself short of a spot to park your towel.

If the shallowness of the constant round of shopping, sunbathing and clubbing leaves you with a feeling of ennui, a more highbrow time can be had at the **Museu d'Art Contemporani** (Museum of Modern Art). Housed in an 18th-century powder store and armoury, the gallery hosts rotating exhibitions of modern art with an emphasis on local artists.
Ronda de Narcìs Puget, Ibiza Town. Tel: (971) 302 723. Open: Oct–Mar Tue–Sun 10am–1.30pm; Apr–Sept Tue–Fri 10am–1.30pm & 5–8pm, Sat & Sun 10am–1.30pm. Admission charge.

80km (50 miles) southwest of Mallorca.

Mallorca

La Seu and the Castell de Bellver are the two edifices that most impose themselves on your view as you approach Palma, Mallorca's capital. Ships dock some distance from the old town. Many cruise lines will organise a shuttle, and a local bus also goes fairly regularly from the road that runs by the port. Otherwise, it's walkable in about half an hour, or you can take one of the expensive taxis.

One of the first package-holiday destinations for Brits, Mallorca has become synonymous with mass tourism. Today it's the most popular, as well as the biggest, of the Balearics. It's true that wandering around the capital, **Palma**, you may be hard pressed to spot the Mallorcan among the legions of tourists, but the city has a charm and history that are often overlooked by its detractors. Ignore the outer reaches of the place, which have suffered from tasteless developments, and stick to the old town, where various invaders and rulers have left their architectural legacies, and a small-town atmosphere survives despite the bustle.

Dominating the town both from land and sea, the cathedral, **La Seu**, is a spectacular presence. If you're not going to Barcelona, a visit here is a chance to see some Gaudí handiwork, as the Catalan architect designed several of the interior aspects.
Plaza de Almoina. No tel. Open: Apr, May & Oct Mon–Fri 10am–5.15pm;

The building of La Seu in Palma began in 1229 but was not finished until 1601

Jun–Sept Mon–Fri 10am–6.15pm;
Nov–Mar Mon–Fri 10am–3.15pm; year-
round Sat 10am–2.15pm. Closed: Sun.
Admission charge.

Aside from the cathedral, the town also has some other monuments and attractions of note, some of which, like the 10th-century **Banys Arabs** (Arab Baths) convey something of the island's colourful history. Otherwise, the pleasure lies in walking through the medieval part of town, and stopping for a drink at one of the many restaurants and cafés that line the main roads.
Banys Arabs. Carrer Serra 7.
Tel: (971) 721 549. Open: Apr–Sept daily
9am–7pm; Oct–Mar daily 9am–6pm.
Admission charge. Bus: 15.

200km (125 miles) south of Barcelona.

Menorca
Whitewashed cliff-side houses herald the
approach of Maó, said to be the second
largest natural deep-water port in the
world. Cruise liners dock at the
commercial port, within easy (albeit
steep) walking distance of the town.

The furthest Balearic Island from the coast of Spain, Menorca remains relatively undeveloped – in comparison with its neighbours. Vegetation abounds, thanks in part to UNESCO, which declared the second largest island of the archipelago a Biosphere Reserve. The classification also recognised the huge preponderance of archaeological sites. A period of British rule has left

The Portal de San Marco in Maó, the Menorcan capital

Menorca with a distinct architectural heritage, and the Georgian style can be traced in some buildings.

The capital, towards the east of the island, is **Maó** (or Mahón in Castillian), and most tourists will pitch up here. You'll find the standard pleasant squares, churches and the odd museum, though the beaches are at a remove from the town. The British naval influence is evident in a lesser spotted Spanish attraction – a gin distillery. Visitors to **Xoriguer Distillery** can see how the spirit is made, before, of course, sampling and buying some.
Moll de Ponent 93, Maó. Tel: (971) 362
197. Open: Mon–Fri 8.30am–7pm, Sat
9am–1pm. Closed: Sun. Free admission.

140km (87 miles) east of Palma de
Mallorca.

Clubbing in Ibiza

Mention Ibiza, and the word 'hedonism' may well spring to mind. The island's clubs are among the most revered in Europe, and many well-established club brands started life on the Balearic Island. So integral has Ibiza been to the modern dance music scene, that Balearic Beat or Balearic House has become an established type of pop music. Meanwhile, A-listers continue to choose the island for their revelry.

Like its Asian equivalent, Goa, the dance scene in Ibiza grew out of the hippy communities that formed here in the 1960s. The island's isolation ensured travellers were treated warmly. Attracted by the low cost of living and laidback island lifestyle, artists and other alternative types began to settle in Ibiza Town and San Carlos. Their full-moon parties soon became the stuff of legend, and the island's reputation took root.

By the 1980s, the scene was established enough to be bringing in top disc jockeys to play Ibiza. When British DJs Trevor Fung, Paul Oakenfold and Danny Rampling were holidaying on the island in 1987, they heard an Argentinian counterpart playing an eclectic style of music that encompassed genres from rock to house. Back in the UK, they

During the 1960s, incoming artists and bohemians settled in quiet old Ibiza Town and started to hold late-night parties

introduced Balearic Beat, as it became known, to a wider audience, feeding into the burgeoning British rave scene. The chilled-out and innovative sounds that emerged from Ibiza made stars of hitherto unknown DJs and spawned myriad Balearic and Ibiza themed compilation albums (invariably featuring tanned, bikini-clad blonde women on the covers).

At the heart of the scene are the super-clubs that bring hordes of revellers flying over each summer. They include Privilege (which, with a capacity of 10,000, claims to be the biggest club in the world), Amnesia (famous for its foam parties, Cream and Manumission club nights) and global brand Pacha. With such cachet, the clubs have played host to the higher echelons of modern celebrity: Madonna, Tom Cruise, Kylie Minogue, Kate Moss and the sultan of Brunei are among the many repeat visitors. Some even have homes on the island.

But Ibiza's relentless rise as a party destination has not pleased everyone. The local government is keen to foster a more sedate, upmarket style of tourism. Clubs have been obliged to close at 6am (the island's indefatigable clubbers would happily go on through the morning), and new hotels now have to be five-star. A Belgian newspaper accused rowdy British tourists of having 'single-handedly ruined the Spanish island

The dance floors at Amnesia can pack in more than 5,000 people

Ibiza', and in 1998 the British vice consul quit his post for the same reason, saying such holidaymakers made him 'ashamed to be British'.

In the meantime, the nightlife continues apace, despite regular debate over whether Ibiza is 'over'. A decrease in numbers of revellers, stricter laws and drugs busts are often tipped to herald the end of the Balearic dance scene. But, as an article in *The Guardian* newspaper pointed out, such comment is nothing new. As early as 1933, German artist Walther Benjamin complained that the island's new noise and crowds had spoiled its appeal for him, while Dutch writer Hans Sleutelaar echoed the same sentiments in 1963. Regardless, the Balearic Beat goes on.

France, Italy and their islands

For many travellers, the South of France and coast of Italy are the heart of the Mediterranean region. Highlights of all kinds repay a stop in this central region of the Med. Culturally, few countries can challenge Italy, the birthplace of the Renaissance, while the South of France is probably unsurpassed for 'lifestyle', encapsulated in its chic Riviera resorts. And gastronomically, both countries can stake a claim to be world leaders.

On top of the grace and good living associated with the country as a whole, France's south coast also has its glorious Mediterranean weather and dazzling beaches going for it. But while equally pleasant and sunny patches of sand can be found around the region, what can never be replicated is the *je ne sais quoi* of the French Riviera. Glitz and glamour bring the great and the good to resorts such as St-Tropez, and Hollywood royalty decamps en masse

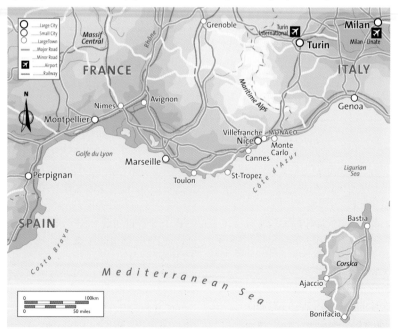

to Cannes once a year for the film festival. Neat, clean streets, chic local couples walking impossibly small dogs and expensive fashion boutiques reaffirm the inescapable Frenchness of the Riviera. And while you sit, enjoying some mussels and a glass of wine at a pavement café, you can be part of it.

Italy's boot shape makes the country ideally suited to exploration by cruise, as most of its important cities are reachable from the coast. No less than France, Italy sums up the good life. Its cultural treasures, such as the art in the Galleria degli Uffizi (Uffizi Gallery) in Florence, are second to none. If your cultural predilections are at the other end of the artistic scale, the country does high fashion and brand names in a big way, and there is fun to be had in perusing the swanky clothes boutiques and car showrooms, regardless of whether your wallet will stretch to a purchase. Italy's architecture is similarly prepossessing, with the Torre pendente di Pisa (Leaning Tower of Pisa) only the quirkiest of a legion of breathtaking buildings. A day's sightseeing will necessitate energy replacement, with pizza and pasta both doing the job admirably. Both France and Italy have beautiful islands, which give a twist to the mainland culture, and are popular cruise stops in their own right.

FRANCE
Marseille
Ships dock in the city's commercial port, from where you can transfer to the city's Vieux Port district by bus, either a laid-on shuttle or a local service. Taxis are available but will probably be costly.

It's definitely not France's poshest coastal city – indeed, Marseille has the sorry reputation of being one of the most crime-ridden towns on the Med. But the city has been unfairly maligned. Like most ports, it feels slightly edgy, and as one of Europe's most ethnically diverse cities, there can be tensions. But the Mediterranean melting pot of cultures also creates an exotic feel, and the city emanates a down-at-heel charm.

Marseille is also home to as many fabulous buildings as you would expect in a major French town, perhaps the most stunning of which is the **Palais Longchamps**. This stately 19th-century palace, also a water tower, contains the **Musée des Beaux Arts** and the **Musée d'Histoire Naturelle** (Museum of Fine Arts and of Natural History respectively), and sits in some superb gardens.

Palais Longchamps. Blvd du Jardin Zoologique. Tel: (491) 138 900. Open: summer Tue–Sun 11am–6pm; winter Tue–Sun 10am–5pm. Musée des Beaux Arts. Tel: (491) 145 930. Open: Oct–May Tue–Sun 10am–5pm; Jun–Sept Tue–Sun 11am–6pm. Admission charge.
Musée d'Histoire Naturelle. Tel: (491) 145 950. Open: summer Tue–Sun 11am–6pm; winter Tue–Sun 10am–5pm. Admission charge.

A novel way of getting around is **Le Petit Train Touristique de Vieux**

France, Italy and their islands

Marseille (*www.petit-train-marseille. com*), which departs from close to where port shuttles drop off. Two different routes take passengers around the city's major sights. These include the basilica **Notre Dame de la Garde.** This neo-Byzantine church that occupies Marseille' highest point is worth seeing both from inside and out. The 60m (200ft) statue of Virgin and Child is visible from land and sea, while the interior decor is an eclectic mix that includes mosaics, murals, war medals, and even football shirts donated by players and fans of Olympique de Marseille.
Tel: (491) 134 080.
www.notredamedelagarde.com.
Open: summer Mon–Sat 7.25am–7.15pm, Sun 8am–7.15pm; shorter hours in winter. Bus: 60.

THE CHÂTEAU D'IF

Built in the 16th century on the tiny island of If at the behest of King François I, the Château d'If's initial *raison d'être* was to repel naval attacks (which never came). However, it gained notoriety not as a fortress but as a prison, where political and religious inmates were abandoned and forgotten. The gaol came to international attention when French writer Alexandre Dumas used it in his revenge novel *The Count of Monte Cristo.* Betrayed by his best friend, hero Edmond Dantès is imprisoned on the isle for 14 years, before escaping and wreaking flamboyant revenge on his enemies. No real person is believed to have managed to replicate the escape. The château is now open to tourists.
Open: Oct–Mar daily 9.30am–5.30pm; Apr–Sept daily 9.30am–6.30pm. Admission charge.

The city is also a gateway to Provence, and cruise lines offer trips to the countryside.

The Palais Longchamps in Marseille houses two museums

Looking out over Toulon harbour from a dockside café

Toulon

Mont Faron and Toulon's old city will be visible on your approach, and you may also spot some warships. Follow the seafront by foot to reach the old town.

France's main Mediterranean naval base for over 300 years, Toulon's strategic importance is evident in the many forts that dot the town. Its role as a port takes precedence over tourism, although there is a cathedral and several museums to visit. The **Mémorial du Débarquement de Provence** (Memorial Museum to the Landings in Provence) is the most unusual of Toulon's selection. Opened by Charles de Gaulle, it covers the 1944 Allied landings in Provence, in which French troops took part.

The base of Mont Faron. Tel: (494) 880 809. Open: Oct–Apr Tue–Sun 9.45am–12.45pm & 2–5.30pm; May & Jun Tue–Sun 9.45am–12.45pm & 2–6pm; Jul–Sept Tue–Sun 9.45am–12.45pm & 1.45–6.30pm. Closed: Mon. Admission charge.

48km (30 miles) southeast of Marseille.

St-Tropez

St-Tropez's small port caters to yachts, not cruise ships, so larger vessels must drop anchor and send their passengers ashore by tender. It's just a short walk into town.

Saint Torpes, the possibly legendary martyr from whom the town takes its name, would no doubt be horrified if he saw what St-Tropez has become. The former pilgrimage site and humble fishing village is now a temple to bling, a playground for the rich and famous

The pretty harbour at St-Tropez

that has given its name to something as frivolous as a tan. First popularised by the French writers and artists of the late 19th and early 20th centuries, St-Tropez's fame was secured (along with that of Brigitte Bardot) with the 1956 film *And God Created Woman*. Stars flocked to snap up houses in the 'Marbella of France', with Elton John and Mick Jagger among others joining Bardot in buying local *pieds-à-terre*. Today's stars continue to frequent the clubs of St Trop, as the cognoscenti refer to it.

This Côte d'Azur resort has no specific must-see attractions; it's more about imbibing the atmosphere and hoping to catch a glimpse of a visiting celebrity. There's plenty of retail therapy, if you have the inclination –

and the credit card – for it. Charming alleyways are peppered with restaurants, interior design boutiques (St-Tropezians must be avid re-decorators) and fashion stores. As throughout the French Riviera, small dogs are *de rigueur* – some owners even accessorise their pooch with shades.

Emerge from the network of alleyways to the harbour, and the pleasant, upmarket atmosphere is confirmed. Prettily coloured houses line the seafront, where a flotilla of expensive yachts and sailing boats bob gently on the glistening Med. There are plenty of restaurants in which to order a plate of mussels, and people-watch. The prices, though not cheap, are not as exorbitant as the calibre of the resort and bank balances of its patrons might suggest.

Don't neglect the old port area, where the laidback atmosphere is in marked contrast to the rest of the town. Here, tourists simply sit and hang out, and it costs nothing. There is a beach nearby, but the better beaches are only reachable on wheels. Most are private and some are for nudist, or at least topless bathers.

63km (39 miles) east of Toulon.

Cannes

The majority of cruise ships are too large to dock in Cannes. If you're brought onshore via tender, the quay is within walking distance of the centre of town; turn right as you exit the terminal. Some ships dock instead at St-Raphaël, from where Cannes is a half-hour train ride.

The star-studded annual film festival (*see pp54–5*) means that Cannes possibly outdoes even its near neighbour St-Tropez in the glamour stakes. Another former fishing village turned playground of the rich and famous, it's similarly full of stylish and expensive boutiques and small dogs. Designer labels abound. So do costly yachts, of which you'll see an abundance at the *Vieux Port*.

To the west of this area is the hill known as **Le Suquet**, where the broad shopping streets are replaced by narrower lanes with a more interesting range of shops and eateries. It is here, in Old Cannes, that you'll find the 12th-century castle containing the **Musée de la Castre**. Its absorbing ethnographical and archaeological exhibits include antiquities from the Mediterranean region, Middle East and beyond. Its hilltop location also affords

pleasant views of the town and bay. *Place de la Castre. Tel: (493) 385 526. Open: Apr–Jun & Sept Tue–Sun 10am–1pm & 2–6pm; Jul & Aug daily 10am–7pm; Oct–Mar Tue–Sun 10am–1pm & 2–5pm. Admission charge.*

This museum, and the other sights around town, will make very pleasant diversions, but most visitors to Cannes are here for the glamour, not for anything educational. Spend some time strolling along the **Boulevard de la Croisette**, which runs from the Palais des Festivals et des Congrès, the home of the Cannes festival, along the seafront. This is where the money is: top hotels, casinos for high-rollers, upmarket boutiques, clubs with strict guest lists, chic little boutiques and galleries – and an armada of yachts in the marina opposite. Once you're tired of walking, there are plenty of private beaches on which to preen – but be prepared to pay for the privilege.

42km (26 miles) northeast of St-Tropez.

Many cruise ships visiting Cannes dock at nearby St-Raphaël

Cannes Film Festival

Bestowing the Midas touch of the movie world, success at Cannes pretty much makes your film a gold-plated hit. The film festival, one of the oldest and most prestigious in the calendar, is equally about the stars, whose dalliances, marital problems, pregnancies, brushes with the law and outfits often make a sideshow of the actual business of rewarding excellent films. Cannes has glamour in spades – even the notoriously scruffy paparazzi don tuxedos for the occasion.

The festival was born in the 1930s in protest against the fascist

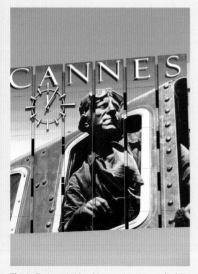

The Italian actor Lino Ventura graces a clock in Cannes

governments of Germany and Italy, who had interfered in the selection procedures of the Venice Film Festival. With support from the UK and US, the French Minister of National Education, Jean Zay, decided to hold an alternative festival. Pipping Vichy, Biarritz and Algiers to the post, Cannes was chosen as the site. Pioneer filmmaker Louis Lumière was all set to preside over the first event, in September 1939, when Germany's invasion of Poland and the outbreak of World War II put paid to the festival before a reel had been shown.

Le Festival International de Cannes finally got its debut in 1946. But things did not initially go smoothly. A secret agreement with Italy to hold their film festivals in alternate years was exposed, to the embarrassment of the French organisers. The next year a storm blew the roof off the venue. Lack of money occasionally meant no festival was held. In 1968 proceedings were interrupted by a group of directors in support of striking students and workers.

But despite the various hiccups, gradually the festival matured, a jury was introduced and the principles of fairness adopted, a commercial aspect brought in, allowing films to be more

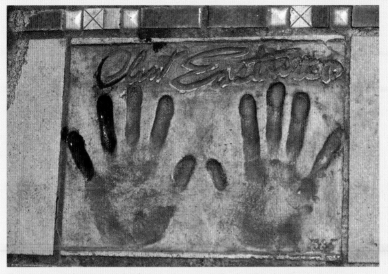

The handprints of Clint Eastwood feature among many on the Allée des Stars in Cannes

effectively traded, then the various sections that comprised later stagings were suggested and implemented. In 1983 a larger, purpose-built venue, the *Palais des Festivals et des Congrès*, was constructed to host the festivities. Today it is surrounded by the cement palm-prints of various luminaries, in the style of those outside Grauman's Chinese Theatre in Hollywood. 'The Bunker,' as the new venue was nicknamed, met with strong disapproval from many.

The main event is the selection of the Palme d'Or, whose title has alternated with the Grand Prix du Festival International du Film as the top prize on offer. Several winners have gone on to become established classics, including *Brief Encounter*, *The Third Man*, *La Dolce Vita*, *Blow-Up*, *Taxi Driver*, *Apocalypse Now* and *Pulp Fiction*. Many other, lower-profile winners have found a global audience thanks to the accolade.

Now perhaps the premier film event in Europe, the Cannes festival has allowed low-budget and niche films the opportunity to succeed, despite their limited box-office receipts. In turn, the event has made its own way onto film. A dozen movies have featured Cannes in their plot. In the fictional realm, the festival has been hijacked by terrorists, used to turn a 'nobody' into a star as a bet, been the scene of a diamond heist, and been ruined by Mr Bean, who managed to screen his own home movies in place of the official film.

Part of the long beach at Nice, with the Promenade des Anglais just above

Nice

If you find yourself sailing towards a palm-fringed quay, that's the Promenade des Anglais, which means you're in Nice and can walk to the sights from the port. Larger vessels tend to anchor in Villefranche, which is a picturesque hillside fishing village. Passengers are brought to shore by tender, and from there buses and trains make the 5km (3-mile) trip to Nice. The bus stop is about a 20-minute walk away from the port, but a minibus also departs from outside the port terminal. The entrance to the train station is at the side of a restaurant up some stairs. From Nice station, follow signs to Promenade des Anglais; from there, the sights are off to the left. There will also be taxis outside the terminal.

Though its name doesn't quite have the cachet of a Cannes or a St-Tropez, Nice is a respectably fashionable Côte d'Azur resort in its own right. More laidback than either of its flashy neighbours, it is a good choice for travellers tired of in-your-face posing and seeking a more relaxed and cultural destination. The old town, **Vieux Nice**, has an exceptional array of attractive buildings, and the influence of Italy, whose border is only around 30km (19 miles) away, is traceable in some of the architecture, particularly in the case of the churches. The narrow streets and colourful houses seem a world away from the designer retail districts elsewhere on the Riviera, while cafés and restaurants offer picturesque surroundings if you choose to stop for a moment's repose.

Nice's shopping is also markedly different from the higher-end Riviera resorts. Cours Saleya, the road running parallel to the Quai des États Unis, is the venue of the daily market. The area between Place Masséna and Vieux Nice is a riot of colour for six days of the week, with flowers and fresh produce on sale (*open for flowers: Tue, Thur & Fri 6am–5.30pm, Wed & Sat 6am–6.30pm, Sun & public holidays 6am–1.30pm; fruit and vegetables, morning only*). On Monday, the perishables give way to antiques (*7.30am–6pm*).

23km (14 miles) northeast of Cannes.

Monaco
While some ships still anchor, and send their passengers to the shore by tender, Monte Carlo's new terminal has allowed more vessels to dock in the port. Whichever is the case, all of the town's points of interest are reachable by foot, though it's a steep climb.

Writer W Somerset Maugham famously labelled Monaco a 'sunny place for shady people', and something about that label is still true. The principality is chiefly known as a tax haven and, with its main attraction being a casino, a whiff off ill-gotten gains still hangs about the place. That doesn't detract at all from its allure – if anything, this shady undercurrent adds a frisson of excitement to a place that is glamorous in the extreme.

As well as rich tax exiles, Monaco and its unofficial capital Monte Carlo are chiefly known for two other things: the royal family and Formula 1. The former (*see box on p58*) is unlikely to

Monte Carlo Casino is approached through formal gardens fringed with palm trees

France, Italy and their islands

THE ROYAL HOUSE OF MONACO

Monaco might be small, but its royal family has a long history: the House of Grimaldi has held power for over seven centuries, since François Grimaldi is said to have disguised himself as a monk to seize the fortress protecting the principality. Today's royals are still in place despite wartime occupation and exile. Now perennial favourites of *Hello* magazine, Prince Rainier sent interest in his clan soaring when he married Hollywood star Grace Kelly. Tragedy and scandal kept the Monaco royals on the front pages. The couple's daughter Princess Stephanie survived a car crash that killed her mother aged 52. She later married one bodyguard, is rumoured to have borne a child by another, then married and divorced a trapeze artist. Sister Caroline is on her third marriage, the second having ended in tragedy when her husband was killed in a boating accident aged 30. The numerous dalliances of their brother Prince Albert, who is now Monaco's ruler, have produced two illegitimate children, but no heir.

impinge on your visit, but if you visit at the right time of year (usually late May), the preparations for the Monaco Grand Prix, the race itself and even its clean-up, can be quite interesting.

At any time of the year, the streets of Monte Carlo are worth walking (not that many of the residents seem to do so – they are far more likely to cruise past in a chauffeur-driven Bentley or Rolls-Royce, or speed by at the wheel of a Ferrari or Maserati). Money is everywhere, which is particularly evident in the brand names of the town's designer stores – Armani, Chanel, Gucci, Prada, Cartier, Ferrari and other stores where the old rule of 'if you have to ask the price, you can't afford it' generally applies. Luxury stores can be found all around town, but there's a cluster on the Avenue des Beaux-Arts.

Money is also the name of the game at the city's centrepiece attraction, the **Monte Carlo Casino**. Perhaps because of its impressive reputation and James Bond associations, the gambling side of the casino is a little disappointing (unless you wangle your way into the high-rollers' poker room), with the typical customer more likely to be a hapless cruise passenger blowing their holiday budget than a suave spy locked in a battle of wills with a mega-villain. But the magnificent Baroque building alone is worth the entry fee. There are some restrictions on dress and on what you can take inside, and you must show your passport when you enter. (This is to keep out under-18s and, strangely, Monégasques, as citizens of Monaco are called, who are forbidden from entering.) Sadly, given the beauty of the building, photography is forbidden. *Place du Casino. Tel: 9216 2000. www.montecarlocasinos.com. Open: daily 2pm–closing, hours may vary. Admission charge.*

For a whistle-stop tour of the other points of interest that avoids climbing (Monte Carlo is on a steep hill), take the 35-minute tour by tourist train from the **Musée Océanographique** (Oceanography Museum). The highly reputed museum and aquarium are also worth a visit in their own right.

Avenue St-Martin. Tel: 9315 3600.
www.oceano.mc. Open: Oct–Mar daily
10am–6pm; Apr–Jun & Sept daily
9.30am–7pm; Jul & Aug daily
9.30am–7.30pm. Admission charge.

13km (8 miles) east of Nice.

Corsica
Ajaccio
Ships dock or anchor to the north end of
the Bay of Ajaccio, from where it's a
pleasant walk, dotted by market stalls,
into town.

The main claim to fame of the fourth
largest island in the Mediterranean is as
the birthplace of Napoleon Bonaparte.
And Corsican entrepreneurs are certainly
not going to let you forget it (think Le
Grand Café Napoléon next to Bonaparte
Cinema, and similar). But there are far

more reasons to visit the Scented Isle (so
named for the aroma of its vegetation)
than the French emperor connection.
Corsica's beaches are frequently cited as
some of the best the Mediterranean has
to offer, which is no small accolade given
that the competition includes the Greek
islands. There's a pleasant languor about
Ajaccio, the island's main city, with its
15th-century citadel, spiky palm trees,
statues and neat, pedestrianised areas.
Birdsong complements the slow pace of
life, while the surrounding hills provide
a picturesque backdrop.

Though the island has a Frenchness
about it, discernible in the wine, meat
and cheese that characterise the small
market located immediately after you
exit the port, it is in fact much closer to
the Italian than the French mainland.
There are subsequently traces of Italy,
too; not only is Italian spoken by many

France, Italy and their islands

One of the statues of Napoleon Bonaparte in Ajaccio

Corsicans, but the Corsican language is itself close to the Tuscan dialect.

The celebration of its most famous son also reaffirms the island's pride in its identity. Unsurprisingly, many of the attractions reference Napoleon to some extent. Tucked down an easily missable alleyway, **Maison Bonaparte** is the (restored) humble dwelling where the emperor was born and grew up.
Rue St Charles. Tel: (495) 214 389;
www.musee-maisonbonaparte.fr.
Open: Apr–Sept Tue–Sun 9am–noon &
2–6pm; Oct–Mar Tue–Sun 10am–noon
& 2–4.45pm. Closed: Mon.
Admission charge.

If your appetite for all things Bonaparte remains unsated, the **Salon Napoléonien** contains further memorabilia.
Hôtel de Ville, Place Foche. Open:
15 Jun–15 Sept Mon–Fri 9–11.45am
& 2–5pm; 16 Sept–14 Jun Mon–Fri
9–11.45am & 2–4.45pm. Closed: Sat,
Sun & public holidays. Admission charge.

230km (143 miles) southeast of Nice.

ITALY
Sardinia
Cagliari
From Cagliari's port, a shuttle bus into
town is usually provided.

With Corsica to the north, mainland Italy off to the east, Tunisia down below and the Balearic Islands lying west, Sardinia was described by D H Lawrence as 'lost between Europe and Africa and belonging to nowhere'. The island – the Mediterranean's second largest – is part of Italy. But having been colonised by a succession of regimes, including the Spanish – thanks to the enviably strategic location of its port – it has a distinct identity aside from its Italian characteristics. It's certainly cleaner than much of the mainland, with pristine beaches one of the main lures for the many tourists (August, in particular, can feel overly crowded). The varied topography also gives rise to opportunities for a number of demanding sports, such as rock-climbing and caving.

Sardinia's main port is also the capital, **Cagliari**. A hospitable city, it's suited to walking and drinking in the Mediterranean atmosphere, possibly in a café. The old centre is called Castello, or 'castle', also the meaning of the town's name in Sardinian. Limestone is the prevailing construction material, and it features in the surviving city walls, which include two white 13th-century towers, Torre di San Pancrazio and Torre dell'Elefante. The effect of the white limestone prompted Lawrence to liken Cagliari to a 'white Jerusalem'. Those who enjoy historical sights will find plenty of eye-catching old buildings, many of which are religious. Art Deco and neoclassicism can be seen in some of the newer structures.

Cagliari has the distinction of boasting one of the longest beaches of any Italian town. Running for over 11km (7 miles), its fine, white sand

France, Italy and their islands

France, Italy and their islands

The 13th-century Torre di San Pancrazio in Cagliari, Sardinia

made Poetto beach popular with both Sardinians and tourists, although the authorities are now struggling against erosion. The beach, 4km (2½ miles) east of the centre, is reachable by bus. Another natural attraction, northwest of Poetto, is the Stagno di Molentargius, from where you might be able to spot the local flamingos.

430km (270 miles) southwest of Rome.

Genoa
The hilly ground around Genoa makes for a pretty approach by cruise ship. Genoa's port is large, so the distance to the town centre depends on where your liner berths. From the port, turn right; the walk into town should take no more than 20 minutes.

Genoa's pretty Old Port

France, Italy and their islands

Part workaday port, part grand old Italian metropolis, Genoa presents a mixture of elegance and grittiness. The country's largest Mediterranean and most important commercial port owes a strong debt to the maritime, not least through its most famous son. Explorer Christopher Columbus, held by some to have 'discovered' America, was born and grew up in Genoa, and is commemorated around the city.

The waterfront area is one of the main districts of interest, particularly following its renovation. The Porto Antico, or Old Port, plays host to attractions nautical and non-nautical. Like most waterfronts, this one is suitable for strolling. A well-run tourist

information office can be found in the vicinity.

A top attraction is the **Acquario di Genova**. Europe's biggest aquarium is an engaging temple to the aquatic world. Its 70 tanks, which are said to contain 4 million litres (900,000 gallons) of water, are home to some 600 different species, including crocodiles, alligators, dolphins, seals and turtles. There's a programme of events, and the emphasis is on conservation. Queues can be long, and it's possible to buy tickets for use later in the day.
Ponte degli Spinola. Tel: (010) 234 5666. www.acquariodigenova.it (Italian only). Open: daily from 8.30, 8.45 or 9.30am–7.30, 8.30 or 10pm (see website). Admission charge.

Away from the sea, Genoa has a large historical district (the city claims it's the biggest in Europe). Though its attractions are not as well known as Pisa's or Florence's, there is certainly an array of impressive edifices, an inheritance from the days when its naval importance made it a hugely prosperous centre of trade. They are not set out as straightforwardly for the visitor as is the case elsewhere, and often you'll find the prettiest building almost secreted down an unlikely looking narrow street. The wonderfully named Piazza de Ferrari, a majestic square set around a fountain, is your starting point for the **Teatro Carlo Felice**, the city's main opera house, and **Palazzo Ducale** (the Doge's Palace), which is now a flourishing arts centre.

Columbus is also said to have been born in a house near here.

Teatro Carlo Felice. Passo Eugenio Montale 4. Tel: (010) 538 1363.
www.carlofelice.it.
Palazzo Ducale. Piazza Matteotti.
Tel: (010) 557 4000.
www.palazzoducale.genova.it.
Open: Tue–Sun 9am–7pm.
Admission charge for exhibitions.

On **Via Garibaldi**, a UNESCO-listed site, other important buildings are to be found. A plethora of *palazzi*, most built in the mid-16th century to house the Genovese elite, embody the Mannerist style of architecture. Some, including the 17th-century **Palazzo Rossi**, now house galleries.

Via Garibaldi 18. Tel: (10) 557 4972.
www.museopalazzorosso.it. Open:

The Palazzo Ducale in Genoa is now an arts centre

Tue–Fri 9am–7pm, Sat & Sun 10am–7pm. Closed: Mon. Admission charge.

Visitors who like art of a religious hue will enjoy the frescoes that adorn both the interior and exterior of several buildings. Even the dead cannot escape the city's art: the 19th-century **Cimitero di Staglieno** (Staglieno Cemetery) boasts numerous marble, stone and bronze statues, monuments, chapels and tombs for its residents, who include British soldiers and some religious groups. The cemetery's size necessitates its own dedicated bus service to get visitors (and mourners) from one part to another. Writers Mark Twain and Evelyn Waugh have both extolled the place.

Piazzale Resasco. Tel: (010) 870 184. Open: daily 7.30am–5pm. Free admission. Bus: 480 & 482 from the Stazione Genova Brignole, 34 from Stazione Principe.

144km (90 miles) northeast of Monaco.

Pisa

From Livorno station, the train goes to Pisa approximately every half-hour, with a journey time of just over 15 minutes. Some local operators also wait at the port to take groups of tourists there by minibus.

It may be the site of one of Italy's most famous universities, plus a host of other dignified and gracious buildings, but Pisa is famous around the world for one thing: a wonky tower. Inept engineering has proved a gift to the

A view of the famous tower, slanting behind a classical urn in Pisa

tourism industry, as legions of curious travellers make their way to the quirky landmark and assume the classic holiday snap pose, with palms aligned with the lower side of the tower, as if supporting it. The number of people allowed up it at any one time is limited, for obvious reasons, so you may have to wait.

Torre pendente di Pisa (Leaning Tower of Pisa). Campo dei Miracoli. www.opapisa.it. Open: from 8.30 to 10am–5 to 8.30pm or later, depending on season (see website). Admission charge.

The Campo dei Miracoli (Square of Miracles) that the tower dominates is home to other constructions of note. The next most striking is the **Duomo di Pisa** (Pisa Cathedral). Construction of the cathedral started in 1063. It was

The Little Venice district of Livorno

built in the Pisan Romanesque style, but aspects of it also betray Byzantine and Muslim aesthetics.

Campo dei Miracoli. www.opapisa.it. Open: Nov–Feb daily 10am–1pm & 2–5pm; early–mid-Mar daily 10am–6 or 7pm; end Mar–Sept daily 10am–8pm; Oct daily 10am–7pm. Admission charge.

140km (87 miles) southeast of Genoa.

Livorno

Depending on precisely where your cruise liner docks, the town centre is either a ten-minute walk (come out onto the main road and turn right) or a bus shuttle away. Taxis wait in the area but tend to eschew short-hop fares and wait for tourists who want to take a costly excursion to Pisa and/or Florence.

Once a key Mediterranean port, today Livorno is often bypassed by cruise passengers heading off for the big-name sights of Pisa and Florence, or the Tuscan countryside. It is true that the Ligurian Sea port lacks the headlining attractions of its near neighbours. But if you have an hour or so to spare after making your way back from further inland, it's a pleasant and laidback place to take in. The relaxation of some laws in the 1580s created an atmosphere of free trade and tolerance that drew in many foreigners including Armenians, Dutch, English, Greeks and Jews, and something of this cosmopolitanism remains. The slightly insalubrious area of Venezia, or Little Venice, lies between the Fortezze Vecchia and Nuova (Old and New Fortresses). Marked by canals, period houses and narrow alleyways, it also merits exploration if you have the time.

15km (9 miles) southwest of Pisa.

Florence

Livorno is the main port from which Florence can be seen on a day trip. From Livorno station (which you can reach by bus from the city centre in ten minutes or so), frequent trains to Florence take around an hour and a half.

The Tuscan capital could fairly lay claim to being Italy's cultural headquarters. Once a republic in its own right, and later the capital of Italy, Florence grew wealthy as a medieval trade and finance hub. The cash-rich city drew in artists and architects, and became known as *la culla del Rinascimento* (the cradle of the Renaissance); another moniker is the Athens of the Middle Ages. Its historical centre is a UNESCO World Heritage Site. Dante, Machiavelli, Galileo and Michelangelo are a few of the cultural big-hitters to be associated with the town.

With such a stellar pedigree and galaxy of world-famous attractions, Florence is inevitably brimming with tourists, and it can often be impossible to spot an Italian, let alone a Florentine. The city centre can be depressingly packed, especially during the warm weather, which is when cruisers are more likely to go. Nonetheless, all the tourist sound and fury cannot detract from the sheer splendour of the buildings, statues and other art on display.

Top of the bill is the **Galleria degli Uffizi** (Uffizi Gallery), which houses one of the world's oldest and most impressive art collections. The artists whose works are inside (there are some statues outside for visitors who don't enter the gallery proper) read like a *Who's Who* of Renaissance art: Raphael,

The busy Piazza della Signoria in Florence

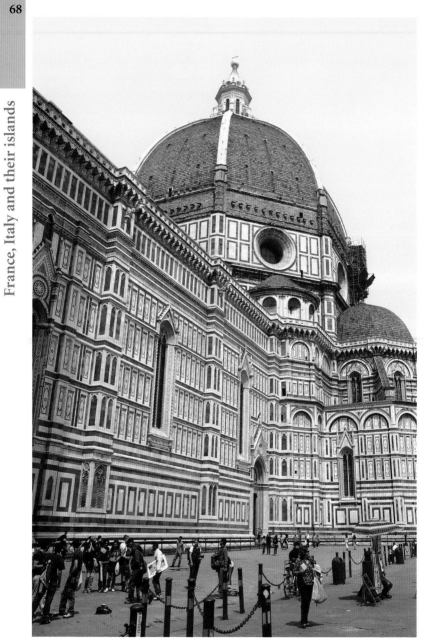

Florence's cathedral, the Basilica di Santa Maria del Fiore

DIVINA COMMEDIA (*DIVINE COMEDY*)

An epic poem and seminal text in world literature, Dante's 14th-century *Divina Commedia* presents the afterlife and its nine circles of hell. The first circle (limbo) receives the virtuous pagans, including most of the Greek poets and philosophers. Next are the lustful, condemned to blow around in a storm. In circle three, gluttons are made to lie in loathsome slush. Then, the greedy and wasteful have to push heavy weights against each other. The angry do battle in the River Styx in the fifth circle, while blazing graves contain heretical sixth circlers. In number seven, all categories of the violent (defined as suicides, criminals, homosexuals, blasphemers and usurers) get a cornucopia of painful punishments. And the eighth and ninth circles see miscreants – from fraudsters and false prophets to pimps, thieves and traitors – undergo myriad fiendish tortures.

Botticelli, Titian, Michelangelo and da Vinci are just the most famous. Queues can be horrendous, and if you're on a short visit, it can make sense to get tickets in advance. Even if you don't go in – and many time-poor cruise passengers don't – the external statues gallery is worth seeing.
Piazza degli Uffizi. Tel: (055) 294 883. www.uffizi.com. Open: Tue–Sun 8.15am–6.35pm. Closed: Mon. Admission charge.

The square to the north of the Uffizi, **Piazza della Signoria**, is crammed with stupendous statues, fountains and buildings including the Palazzo Vecchio (Old Palace), seat of the city's government.

Another major sight is the **Basilica di Santa Maria del Fiore**, Florence's

duomo, or cathedral. It is distinctive for its dome, designed by Filippo Brunelleschi, as it is the largest masonry dome in the world and an emblematic Renaissance project. For superb city views, the cupola can be climbed.
Piazza del Duomo. www.operaduomo. firenze.it. Open: Mon–Wed & Fri 10am–5pm, Thur 10am–4.30pm, Sat 10am–4.45pm or 3.30pm on first Sat of month, Sun & religious holidays 1.30–4.45pm. Free admission.

On a smaller scale, the **Museo Casa di Dante** is not actually the Florentine poet's former house as its name suggests, but a century-old museum built to commemorate his life and work. The paraphernalia on show includes some editions of the *Divina Commedia* (*see box*).
Via Santa Margherita 1. Tel: (055) 219 416. www. museocasadidante.it (Italian only). Open: Apr–Sept Tue–Sun 10am–6pm; Oct–Mar Tue–Sun 10am–5pm. Admission charge.

78km (49 miles) northeast of Livorno.

Civitavecchia
The port, which lies to the north of the town, is not a great distance from the action, but many liners operate a shuttle service.

Civitavecchia, whose name translates to 'ancient town', was built in AD 106 at the behest of the Roman emperor Trajan, who saw its potential to serve as a port for Rome. On today's cruise circuit, it's a role that the Tyrrhenian Sea port still plays. The enormous **Forte Michelangelo**, on the coast to the south of the port, is Civitavecchia's most distinct attraction, but it's unlikely to detain the majority of tourists, who will head straight for the Italian capital. If you've seen Rome before, and wish to stay local, the town's greenery and handsome villas make it a pleasant place for a mooch.

80km (50 miles) northwest of Rome.

Rome

Several trains depart Civitavecchia for Rome every hour, taking between 50 minutes and 1 hour 20 minutes. From the terminus in Rome, many of the main sights are within easy reach.

Its surfeit of nicknames – *Caput Mundi* (Capital of the World), *l'Urbe* (the City), *la Città Eterna* (the Eternal City) are just a sample – give some idea of Rome's importance on the world stage. It is difficult to overplay the history, mythology, architecture and culture that the city encapsulates, or to exaggerate its role in the development of Western civilisation. Rome's major attractions are known (by name, if not in detail) to almost everyone.

Colosseo (the Colosseum)

The 1st-century Colosseo is the largest amphitheatre built under the Roman Empire, and a glorious example of Roman engineering. In half a century of usage, it saw everything from gladiatorial combat and executions to battle re-enactments and drama, in front of baying crowds of up to 50,000 people.
Piazza del Colosseo. Tel: (06) 3996 7700. Open 9am–dusk. Admission charge. Metro: Colosseo.

The Colosseum, floodlit at night

An aerial view of St Peter's Square, Vatican City

Fontana di Trevi (Trevi Fountain)

The largest of Rome's Baroque fountains is a dramatic depiction of scenes from mythology, the star of which is Neptune, god of the sea. The custom of throwing a coin into the fountain (the inspiration for the 1954 film and song *Three Coins in the Fountain*) currently nets €3,000 a day, which subsidises a supermarket for the city's poor.

Piazza dei Trevi. Metro: Barberini.

Scalinata della Trinità dei Monti (Spanish Steps)

Built in 1723–5, the Spanish Steps (so named because they emanated from the Spanish Embassy) used to attract aspiring artists' models, and today you will still find pretty Italian boys and girls showing off, albeit among the legions of tourists. You can sit on the steps, but don't take a picnic – the authorities have banned it. At the foot of the stairs is the pink house where poet John Keats died, now a museum dedicated to him.

Between Piazza di Spagna (at the bottom) and Piazza Trinità dei Monti. Metro: Spagna.

Stato della Città del Vaticano (Vatican City)

This quirk of a state within a city will interest Catholics and non-Catholics alike. The breathtaking Basilica di San Pietro in Vaticano (St Peter's Basilica) and the Cappella Sistina (Sistine Chapel) are two of the top tourist draws.

Northwest Rome. Tel: (06) 6988 5518. www.vatican.va. Limited areas are open to tourists. Admission charge for museums. Metro: Stazione Vaticana.

190km (118 miles) northwest of Naples.

Walk: Rome

Attempting to boil Rome down into a bite-size day trip is a futile exercise (this is a city that takes weeks, not hours, to get to know). But the following will take you to some of the major sights – without entirely exhausting you.

Leave half a day to be able to take in the sights at your leisure.

The walk starts at Stazione Termini, which is one option for disembarkation if you're coming from Civitavecchia by train (and, being a terminus, an easy one not to miss!). Exit the station onto Piazza del Cinquecento, and turn left onto Via Cavour. Take the fifth road on the left and you'll see an ancient Catholic basilica, also on your left.

1 Basilica di Santa Maria Maggiore (St Mary Major)

The best preserved of the four papal basilicas, St Mary Major merits a visit for the fabulous frescoes and mosaics alone. In the Borghese Chapel, a very early icon of the Virgin and Child is displayed. The basilica has been restored and extended, but the original building dates from the 5th century.

Open: daily 7am–7pm. Free admission, but suggested donation.

Carry on along Via Cavour. It will veer slightly to the right, after which go left along Via degli Annibaldi, which brings you out at the Colosseum.

2 Colosseo (Colosseum)

This extraordinary amphitheatre is described in more detail on p70. If you don't have the time or energy to visit, it is still impressive from the outside (although the young men dressed as gladiators who charge tourists for pictures are better avoided, unless your tastes veer towards the kitsch).

Take the large street, Via dei Fori Imperiali, that runs northwest from the Colosseum, which affords views of the Forums of Trajan, Augustus and Nerva on the right. The National Monument to Victor Emmanuel II is at the end of the road on the left.

3 Monumento Nazionale a Vittorio Emanuele II (National Monument to Victor Emmanuel II)

The first king of Italy (the chap on the horse) is honoured at this marble memorial, a splendid construction with Corinthian columns (sometimes called 'the false teeth'), fountains and a couple of goddesses.

Continue in the same direction (the road becomes Via del Corso). After several turn-offs, go left into Via del Seminario, which leads to the Pantheon.

4 Pantheon

Ancient Rome's hardiest relic, the Pantheon was built as a temple to all the gods of Rome. Its extraordinary dome has inspired copycat versions around the world.

Open: Mon–Sat 8.30am–7.30pm, Sun 9am–6pm, weekday holidays 9am–1pm. Free admission.

Return the way you came and continue along Via del Corso until you reach Via delle Muratte, which leads to the Trevi Fountain.

5 Fontana di Trevi (Trevi Fountain)

For further information on the fountain, *see p71.*

Go north past the fountain and join the Via del Tritone, turning right. You will shortly reach Via dei Due Marcelli. Follow it to the Spanish Steps.

6 Scalinata della Trinità dei Monti (Spanish Steps)

Spend some time hanging out with the beautiful people (and recovering from the walk!) on Europe's most iconic staircase. For more information on the steps, *see p71.*

Walk down the Via Sistina and turn left at Via Cavour to return to the station.

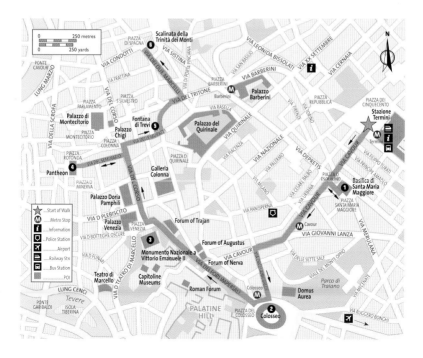

Naples

A couple of castles herald your approach to Naples. Whether the ship docks, or anchors and tenders its passengers to shore, you will be deposited close to the town. Simply cross Via Cristoforo Colombo (although perhaps simply is not the right adverb, given that the traffic on this street is frenetic even by Italian standards!).

Grimy, chaotic, and with the reputation of being a thief's paradise and a pedestrian's nightmare, Naples is certainly not for everyone. While it's a popular port of call on Mediterranean cruise routes, this seems to be more for its location than its inherent allure. But its historic centre is UNESCO listed, and the city does have a certain Latin verve to it. And there is also its culinary pedigree: Naples is credited with being the birthplace of the pizza, with the Neapolitan named after the Campanian port. The city also serves as the gateway to the Amalfi Coast.

Naples is an easy city to walk around, with its main sights within 15 minutes' walk of the port. Medieval, Renaissance and Baroque architecture are the predominant themes. A stroll around **Spaccanapoli**, the main street that scythes through the city's old centre, will yield more beautiful buildings than Naples' grittiness might suggest. (Spaccanapoli, whose name translates to 'Naples splitter', is now known more prosaically as Via Benedetto Croce.)

At a slight remove from the main cluster of old town sights is the

The triumphal arch of the Castel Nuovo in Naples

Duomo (cathedral), a 13th-century structure with a 19th-century façade. An intriguing event at the church is the twice-annual bringing out and liquefying of a vial of blood belonging to St Januarius. The frescoes and artwork of the interior are exceptional. *Via Duomo 147. Tel: (081) 449 097; www.duomodinapoli.it. Open: Mon–Sat 8am–12.30pm & 4.30–7pm, Sun 8am–1.30pm & 5–7pm. Free admission.*

Close to the port, another striking building is the sizeable **Castel Nuovo** (New Castle). Work started on the so-called New Castle in 1279, since when it has been extended and renovated on several occasions. Drama of various kinds was played out here, from papal resignations and elections to sackings by the French and Hungarians, and even treason. It has also been a royal residence. Locals refer to the place as Maschio Angioino, and it is now used for civic business.

Piazza Municipio. Tel: (081) 795 5877, (081) 795 2003. Open: Mon–Sat 9am–7pm. Admission charge.

190km (118 miles) southeast of Rome.

Pompeii

Public and private trains go to Pompeii from the nearby modern-day town of Pompei. From Naples, take the Circumvesuviana, a special service which, as its name suggests, follows the base of Mount Vesuvius. Alight at Pompeii Scavi, 100m (110yds) from the site.

The buried city of Pompeii is a popular excursion with cruise passengers docking in Naples. Along with the lesser-known town of Herculaneum, the Roman city was devastated and entirely buried when Mount Vesuvius erupted in AD 79. Pompeii lay undiscovered for 17 centuries, before it was unearthed entirely by accident. Subsequent painstaking archaeological excavation has yielded fascinating information about life under the Roman Empire at its zenith. An amphitheatre, swimming pool, theatres, restaurants, houses, villas, baths, frescoes, graffiti and inscriptions (one, found above a business reading *Salve, lucru*, translating to 'welcome, money') were among the discoveries that threw light on the life and times of Pompeii. Spaces in the ash, which bodies had occupied, were used to create plaster casts of some of the victims.

The ruins of Pompeii with Mount Vesuvius in the background

France, Italy and their islands

MOUNT VESUVIUS

Europe's only mainland volcano to have erupted within the past century is also considered to be one of the world's most dangerous – thanks to its continued activity and because three million people live in its vicinity. It is best known for destroying the Roman town of Pompeii, but in fact that was not the biggest of its eruptions, and several other settlements also met their end in the same way. Ash from the volcano has previously coated the whole of Southern Europe, reaching as far as Istanbul.

The volcano was created by the collision of the African and Eurasian tectonic plates. Both the Greeks and Romans held it to be sacred, and it has captivated writers, thinkers and scientists alike. Pliny the Elder's fascination with it proved fatal: he breathed in noxious fumes when observing it in action. Mount Vesuvius has not erupted since 1944 – but a huge emergency evacuation plan is on standby for when it does.

Today the city is a UNESCO World Heritage Site, and a chief tourist draw for Italy. Around 2.5 million people visit the site every year, with tickets now including Herculaneum and Stabiae to spread the tourists out in an attempt to alleviate the pressure on Pompeii. Fewer parts of the site are open to the public now than used to be the case, but you could still spend many days exploring here.
Tel: (081) 857 5347. www.pompeiisites.org.
Open: Apr–Oct daily 8.30am–7.30pm, with last tickets sold at 6pm; Nov–Mar daily 8.30am–5pm, with last tickets sold at 3.30pm. Admission charge.

24km (15 miles) southeast of Naples.

Sicily
Palermo
Ships dock around a ten- or fifteen-minute walk from the centre of Palermo. Be wary of potential rogues in the port area.

Sicily's history has made it something of a showcase for the great regimes of the Mediterranean region. Its strategic location – at the 'toe' of Italy's boot, pretty much slap bang in the middle of the Mediterranean – and the fact that it is the largest island, made it of interest to all the great empires of the region. In ancient times, it was part of Magna Graecia, colonised by the Greeks, before becoming the Romans' first province outside their own peninsula. The Vandals and Goths had their turns in control before the island was subsumed by the Byzantine Empire. There followed periods under Islamic, Norman and Spanish rule until Sicily finally became part of Italy in 1860. Though distinctly Italian in feel, the smorgasbord of foreign rulers has also left an architectural mark.

Geologically, the island is dominated by Mount Etna. Europe's biggest active volcano, on the east coast, is also one of the most active in the world, and its fertile volcanic soil feeds much of the island's agriculture.

Sicily's capital, Palermo, no longer enjoys the status it was accorded between the 9th and 12th centuries, as the richest and grandest city in Europe. Though the reverse is now the case in some places – in parts Sicily is poverty-

One side of Palermo's elaborate Quattro Canti square

stricken – the surviving buildings of its heyday and European Union funds are combining to restore some of the lustre.

One example of the varied architectural legacy is the **Quattro Canti** (Four Corners). Officially named Piazza Vigliena, this Baroque square is the intersection of Via Maqueda and the Corso Vittorio Emanuele. An early example of European town planning on a large scale, the square (though technically it's an octagon) was created at the behest of Viceroy the duke of Maqueda at the beginning of the 17th century. The four sections of street alternate with four Baroque buildings, which feature fountains, and on the upper floors statues of the four seasons, four Spanish kings of Italy and four patronesses of Palermo. A little to the south, Piazza Pretoria is home to **Fontana Pretoria**, fashioned by

Florentine sculptor Francesco Camilliani in the mid-16th century. Initially designed for a private home, not for public consumption, the flamboyant fountain is a riot of activity. The several nudes so shocked the Palermo public that the feature became known as Fontana della Vergogna (Fountain of Shame).

The area is also home to other Baroque buildings and a slew of churches. Chief among them is the **Duomo** (cathedral), an enormous and imposing church whose original Norman structure has been embellished with Renaissance and Gothic addenda in the years since construction. Much of the notable architecture around town is Norman, thanks to the Normans' long reign on the island.

Corso Vittorio Emanuele. Tel: (091) 334 373. www.cattedrale.palermo.it (Italian

Two bishops stand guard over their cathedral in Palermo

*only). Open: daily 7am–7pm.
Free admission.*

Though after a wander through Palermo you may feel that you've had your fill of churches, it's worth going the extra mile and factoring in a visit to the 12th-century Duomo in nearby **Monreale**. The astonishing golden mosaics, including a 20m (65ft) high Jesus, are well worth the 16km (10-mile) round trip, and will reanimate any traveller suffering from Mediterranean church fatigue.

Piazza Guglielmo il Buono, Monreale. Tel: (091) 640 4413. Open: daily approximately 9am–12.30pm & (in summer only) 3–7pm. Admission charge. Bus: 389 from Piazza Indipendenza.

307km (191 miles) south of Naples.

Messina

Messina's port can handle cruise liners only up to a certain size, so larger vessels visiting the town will have to anchor off one of the port's jetties and send passengers ashore with a tender service. The town centre is close enough to walk to.

Beleaguered Messina was devastated by an earthquake a century ago, then battered by bombs during World War II, largely depriving it of the architectural legacy other Sicilian cities enjoy. That is not to say that there is no building of note in Sicily's third largest city, located on the northeast of the island. The **Duomo**, originally constructed during the latter part of

The city of Messina and its harbour

the 12th century, and extensively rebuilt post-earthquake and war, houses the largest astronomical clock in the world, made in 1933. Perhaps aware that the restoration could deter tourists, the church authorities have installed quirky animated figures that tell historical stories when the clock strikes noon.

Piazza del Duomo. Tel: (090) 675 175. Open: daily 8am–12.30pm & 4–7pm.

Most tourists choose to leave the city itself for a tour of **Mount Etna** (given that it is still active, you won't actually reach the summit!). The other main excursion option is to **Taormina**, on the east coast of Sicily. Long a popular holiday destination, the resort also has a strong cultural tradition, with several arts festivals over the summer season.

193km (120 miles) east of Palermo.

The history of the Mafia

Offers that cannot be refused. Sleeping with the fishes. Shakedowns. The code of silence: *omertà*. Though few people will ever have come into contact with the Mafia, its rules, traditions and argot are part of the cultural landscape. Since originating in Sicily in the middle of the 19th century, the organisation has become a billion-dollar business and a mainstay of crime film and fiction.

While some historians trace the development of the Sicilian Mafia as far back as medieval times, the general consensus is that it originated in the chaos that followed the Revolutions of the Italian states in 1848. Distinct local bands of outlaws took advantage of the disorder to destroy evidence of their crimes, and eliminate police and informers. The establishment of a new government

The countryside west of Palermo, the type of land where the Mafia first took root

put an end to this, and the gangs were forced to hone their methods, moving into the 'protection' of local estates, and collaborating to safeguard operations.

Papal hostility to the State encouraged Catholic Sicilians to accept the Mafia's code of *omertà*, non-cooperation with the police, while the gangs built up funds from protection rackets, bribery of state officials and cattle rustling. As they formalised, Masonic traditions informed their new rites. Under fascism, Mafiosi were prosecuted with greater zeal, and many fled to the USA, taking their 'occupation' with them. Locally, the Mafia resurrected itself after World War II – some say with tacit US approval owing to their shared anti-communist stance. The Sicilian Mafia were by now thinking and operating internationally, collaborating with the Corsican mob to form an international heroin-trafficking network, first in Europe and then around the globe.

The early 1980s were a period of widespread conflict and killing within the Sicilian Mafia, which became known as The Great Mafia War. Over a thousand murders took place, not only of mobsters but also of

Palermo's Piazza della Memoria commemorates Mafia prosecutor Giovanni Falcone, who was assassinated by the Mafia in 1992 along with his wife and three bodyguards

politicians, police chiefs and magistrates. Afterwards, the new movers and shakers took the organisation in a new direction, with white-collar crime replacing old-school racketeering.

But a disgruntled mobster called Tommaso Buscetta, his position weakened in the war, became the first big *pentito*, convicting hundreds of Mafiosi with his testimony in the Maxi Trial. More killings followed. When two anti-Mafia magistrates were murdered, public revulsion led to a swift crackdown. More informers came forward (often effectively signing the death warrant for family members, when their police protection meant revenge could not be meted out directly). The Mafia turned to terrorism, planting bombs in popular Italian tourist resorts.

When Salvatore Riina, the Godfather who presided over this turmoil, was arrested in 1993, he was replaced by Bernardo Provenzano. A less belligerent boss, his reign, which lasted until his arrest in 2006, heralded a quieter era, allowing the organisation to regroup and regain its potency. Though it lost much of its drugs trade to a rival criminal group, today its tentacles still reach far, with top judges and politicians, including Prime Minister Silvio Berlusconi, accused of having links with the Mafia. Meanwhile, it is bucking the economic downturn as one of Italy's biggest businesses, with a turnover of over $120 billion a year.

Venice

It's worth being on deck for your approach to Venice, as the ship will pass some spectacular views before docking. Ships berth at either the Stazione Marittima (take bus 6 to the east of town) or San Basilio terminal, which is a little further away (vaporetto 61, 62 or 82). A third possibility is Riva dei Sette Martiri – you can walk from here.

Rivalling Rome for the amount of nicknames it has amassed, Venice is truly a special place. Queen of the Adriatic, City of Water, Bridges and Light, the capital of Veneto is an almost surreally pretty sight to behold. Made up of 118 islands in a saltwater lagoon, connected by over 400 bridges, Venice is synonymous with its canals, and transport comes in the form of the gondola, the traditional sculling boat with its associations of moonlight and romance. At least, it does for tourists. Locals going about their day-to-day business are far more likely to be seen in motorised waterbuses called vaporetti, with the gondola tending to be the preserve of tourists, or used for special occasions such as weddings. There are also water taxis, which are a costly but convenient way of getting around.

The two main criticisms of Venice are that it has too little authenticity and too many tourists. Such an extraordinary looking place draws in travellers – and romantics – from all over the world. This, say the critics, has priced the Venetians out of living in their own town, sent prices rocketing and quality plummeting. It is certainly true that Venice can be costly and crowded. But if you're prepared to deviate from the beaten track, it's still possible to find some privacy and seclusion. And, as for the prices, a glance around will show you what you're paying for.

After its foundation in the 5th and 6th centuries, Venice rose to the status of republic, and managed to retain its independence for a millennium. Its location as an Adriatic port put it in prime position for Mediterranean trading routes. By the 13th century it was the richest city in Europe. A costly war, the naval discoveries of Spain and Portugal and the Black Death sent Venice into a decline and it finally fell to Napoleon in 1797. This only accelerated its decay. But though many of its fine palaces were abandoned and neglected, the city has retained enough grandeur to enchant travellers today.

Piazza San Marco

Napoleon is said to have described Piazza San Marco (St Mark's Square) as 'the finest drawing room in Europe'. Hugely popular with tourists and photographers, it is Venice's main piazza, and the only square to be referred to as a piazza (the others are mere *campi*). Topped and tailed by the former Procuratie Vecchie and Procuratie Nuovo (Old Procurators' Offices and the New Procurators' Offices), the piazza now hosts upmarket shops and cafés. But its main point of interest is the **Basilica di San Marco** (St Mark's Basilica). The city's sumptuous cathedral is Byzantine in design, and will instantly call to mind Aya Sofya, if you are familiar with Istanbul. Ships returning from journeys to the Far East brought decorations removed from other structures, making the church a patchwork of different styles. These additions of statues, mosaics and the like add to the building's appeal.

Piazza San Marco. www.basilicasanmarco.it. Open: Nov–Easter Mon–Sat 9.45am–5pm, Sun & holidays 2–4pm; Easter–Nov 9.45am–5pm, Sun & holidays 2–5pm. Admission to church free, admission charge for museum.

Adjoining the church is **Palazzo Ducale**. The official residence of the Doge of Venice (chief magistrate), this Gothic palace was built largely in the 14th and early 15th centuries. A regal-looking construction, it has arcading and an elegant carved marble façade. The palace has classical elements, and is connected to the Bridge of Sighs.

Open: Apr–Oct 9am–7pm, Nov–Mar 9am–5pm. Admission charge.

Ponte del Sospiri (Bridge of Sighs)

Venice's best-known canal crossing, the Bridge of Sighs – like all good bridges do – has its own legend. And this being Venice, it is a romantic one: if lovers kiss on a gondola as it passes below the limestone bridge at sunset, they are guaranteed eternal love. Its history is less charming: the bridge connected prisons with interrogation rooms. The poet Bryon conferred on it the title 'Bridge of Sighs', theorising that the inmates would sigh as they had their final glimpse of Venice before incarceration or execution. However, by the time the bridge was built, the cells (which once held Casanova) in fact contained mostly minor offenders who would certainly have been able to see the city again.

Behind the Palazzo Ducale.

392km (244 miles) northwest of Split.

The Torre dell'Orologio and pigeons in St Mark's Square, Venice

Walk: Venice

The absence of the chaotic traffic that mars many Italian cities makes walking in Venice a delight. The other favoured tourist option is to travel by gondola, but prohibitive prices usually make this a brief, one-off experience, not a general means of transport – unless your holiday fund runs very deep.

Leave half a day in order to be able to take your time.

The walk starts at the city's main square, Piazza San Marco.

1 Piazza San Marco

There is barely a direction you can face in Piazza San Marco without a

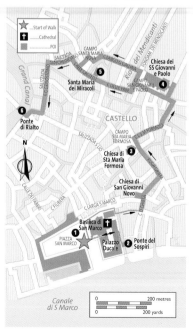

stupendous building in your line of sight. The specifics are listed on *pp82–3*. Just behind the Palazzo Ducale is the Bridge of Sighs.

2 Ponte del Sospiri (Bridge of Sighs)

A tour of the Palazzo Ducale enables you to walk over the famous bridge (*see p83*).

Return to the piazza, and leave by the exit to the north of the basilica. Walk forward, then turn left into Calle della Chiesa. Continue past the Chiesa di San Giovanni Novo and keep going until you hit Ruga Giuffa. Turn left and continue until the Campo Santa Maria Formosa.

3 Campo Santa Maria Formosa

Do this walk on a weekday morning, and you will find a lively little fresh-produce market taking place in the square. The other main attraction is the church: it replaces an original that had an unusual town-planning origin – 7th-century St Magno had a vision

and followed a cloud to this spot, where the church was subsequently built. Part Renaissance, part Byzantine, the place is also worth visiting for its two excellent paintings: Bartolomeo's *Madonna of the Mercy*, and Palma Il Vecchi's *Santa Barbara*. The district, Castello, is renowned for its architectural variety.
Church. Open: Mon–Sat 10am–5pm, Sun 1–5pm. Admission charge.
Exit the square by Calle Lunga Santa Maria Formosa, go left at the end and cross two waterways. Turn left at the end and you'll reach Campo San Giovanni e Paolo.

4 Chiesa dei SS Giovanni e Paolo
Church lovers are spoiled for choice in Venice, but the Chiesa dei SS Giovanni e Paolo is something special. Started by the Dominican Friars, it is a large Italian Gothic-style building made of brick. Top attraction is the largest stained-glass window in Venice, but there are fine tombs and artwork aplenty.
Church. Tel: (41) 523 7510/5913. Open: Mon–Sat 9.30am–7pm, Sun 1–7pm. Admission charge.
Either of the streets that cross the canal Rio dei Mendicanti, Calle Larga Giacinto Gallina and Calle Delle Erbe, will take you to Campo Santa Maria Nova.

5 Santa Maria dei Miracoli
Also known as the 'marble church', this striking late-15th-century church is Venetian Renaissance in design, and full of superb paintings and sculpture, features and detail inside and out.

The early 17th-century Ponte del Sospiri

Church. Open: Mon–Sat 10am–5pm, Sun 1–5pm. Admission charge.
Leave the church and go right along Calle Castelli, left onto Salizzada San Chianciano and left again onto Salizzada San Giovanni Grisostomo. Turn right, then left to reach the Rialto Bridge.

6 Ponte di Rialto (Rialto Bridge)
The oldest bridge across Venice's Grand Canal has stood for over four centuries.
Round off the walk with some shopping at one of the nearby markets, or recover at one of the many cafés in the area.

Dalmatian Coast, Greece and Turkey

Though you will still find pretty beaches, fine Mediterranean cuisine and a profusion of cultural sights, the eastern part of the region has its own distinct flavour. There is little evidence nowadays of the tribulations of the Balkans region in the 1990s, but you may at times still detect a frisson of unpredictability, or a slight nod to the cultures further east.

The Greek islands are among the most laidback places you can find. It's possible to wander along cobblestone alleys, amid whitewashed cottages, seeing nobody but a lethargic cat and hearing nothing but the chiming of a distant church bell. Local people are old hands at the tourism game, and there will be plenty of tavernas where the raki and hospitality flow (sometimes even to the strains of *Zorba the Greek*). If you want your *Shirley Valentine* moment, you will be able to find it. Greece's formidable array of historical sites, some of the most famous in the world, barely require introduction.

The beautiful Dalmatian Coast, here at Cavtat

Diocletian's Palace dates from the early 4th century AD

Turkey might not have been on the holiday circuit for quite as long as its neighbour, or be blessed with so many idyllic islands, but it is now firmly established in the consciousness of the travelling public. Indeed, the country has had its popularity boosted by economics: when currency rate fluctuations make travelling in the Eurozone prohibitive, cheap Turkey is the winner. It shares Greece's heat and beaches, and also lays claim to its fair share of cultural attractions.

Croatia is more of a Johnny-come-lately to cruise itineraries; indeed, it was only established as a country in the 1990s. Consequently, a day spent in one of the two ports on the Dalmatian Coast can be a fascinating introduction to an – as yet – relatively untouristy area. Its geography ensures plenty of fine coastline, charming secluded bays and fishing villages, while there is enough history and culture here to have got UNESCO involved.

CROATIA
Split

Split's port is right by the town centre. Buses and taxis depart from the port to the surrounding areas, such as the Roman town of Salona (open: daylight hours; admission charge), 5km (3 miles) away.

Split, with its pretty historic centre listed as a UNESCO World Heritage Site, is Croatia's largest coastal port. Although its drab suburbs leave a lot to be desired, the sites in the heart of town more than merit Split's inclusion on the cruise circuit. Pavement cafés and restaurants have sprung up along Riva, the waterfront area. With its palm trees, it makes a pleasant place for people-watching or promenading. But the main event is **Dioklecijanova Palača** (Diocletian's Palace), built at the turn of the 4th century AD by the emperor of the same name for his retirement. Fabulously preserved, the palace at one time could hold 9,000 people. The marble and limestone edifice garnered little attention in the West, until the Scottish architect Robert Adam had the ruins surveyed and drew on them for his neoclassical designs. Much of the palace has been given over to homes and businesses. Entrance is through the bronze gates. Split also has a few museums and art galleries worth a look. *Obala Hrvatskog Narodnog Preporoda. Basement open: summer 8am–8pm; winter 8am–noon & 4–7pm. Admission charge.*

392km (244 miles) southeast of Venice.

Dubrovnik

Dubrovnik's old harbour, right below the historical centre, receives some vessels, but most cruise liners dock at the Port of *Gruz, about 4km (2½ miles) to the northwest. Limited space means that if too many ships are in port at the same time, some will drop anchor and tender guests to shore, a pleasant way to view the bay. Once ashore, the old town is a ten-minute taxi journey or bus ride, or, if you have the energy, an enjoyable uphill walk.*

This Adriatic Sea port has no shortage of illustrious fans. George Bernard Shaw said, 'If you want to see heaven on earth, come to Dubrovnik.' Agatha Christie took his advice to heart and honeymooned in a city that was to Lord Byron the 'pearl of the Adriatic'.

Dubrovnik's allure is its unique architecture and design. The 12th-century walled city contains the legacy of the port's maritime supremacy and trade. Squares paved with marble,

The 12th-century walled city of Dubrovnik is a UNESCO World Heritage Site

palaces, churches, monasteries and fountains have come through the battering they received from the Serbs, to hint at Dubrovnik's prosperous yet problematic past. The city has also led a rich artistic life, attracting writers, painters, scientists and thinkers. Today, several museums pay testament to this cultural heritage. Beyond this, there is the simple aesthetic pleasure of the glorious Adriatic views that the city's elevated position affords.

One of Dubrovnik's best-known attractions is the 15th-century **Onofrijeva Cesma** (Onofrio Fountain). On the opposite side of the road is the impressive **Franjevacki Samostan**, or Franciscan Monastery. The 15th-century complex contains one of Europe's oldest working pharmacies, which has been dispensing medication since 1317. The archaic equipment on display offers an intriguing glimpse into the history of medicine; other items related to the city's history can also be seen. The monastery has a bell tower and cloister. *Placa. Tel: (20) 321 497. Open: summer 9am–6pm, hours vary the rest of the year. Admission charge.*

Another important religious edifice is **Crkva Sv Vlaha** (Church of St Blaise). The original Romanesque construction was destroyed in the 1667 earthquake, with the current replacement dating from the early 18th century. The Italian Baroque building is dedicated to Dubrovnik's patron saint, whose likeness can be seen in engravings around the city.

The 14th-century Franciscan Monastery on the Placa, Dubrovnik

Luža Trg. Open: 8am–noon & 4.30–7pm. Free admission.

One of the joys of Dubrovnik is walking around the **fortified walls** that enclose the city (*summer 9am–7.30pm, reduced hours in winter*), entrances to which are at, or close to, Pile Gate, the Dominican Monastery and Fort John. The formidable walls, 2km (1¼ miles) long and in places 25m (82ft) high, are one of the city's chief sources of pride. You'll be treated to excellent views of both the city and the Adriatic Sea. Dubrovnik's surroundings include attractive countryside and islands to visit. *Tourist office: Dubrovačkih branitelja 7. Tel: (20) 427 591. www.tzdubrovnik.hr*

165km (103 miles) southeast of Split.

Greek mythology

The body of stories that the Ancient Greeks built up around their gods and heroes, the world, its origin and nature, and much of their own culture and rituals, still plays a significant role in modern culture and language. Phrases still familiar today include Trojan horses, Achilles' heels and Greeks bearing gifts.... Though dismissed as largely fictional by critics including Plato, many people of the time took them at face value.

A 1st-century BC statue of the goddess Athena, who, according to Homer, fought against Ares during the Trojan War

Initially passed down as spoken poems, it was the written versions produced by Homer and his contemporaries and successors that brought the stories to world prominence. Many of the stories concern the doings of gods and goddesses. Chief among them was Zeus, the king of the gods who lived on Mount Olympus, Greece's highest peak. The god of the sky and thunder, he spent much of his time on matters amorous, and sired a number of gods himself. Zeus gave his favours to fellow gods, mortals and nymphs alike. His powers also extended to dispensing justice and punishment, killing people, turning them into stone or eagles, blinding and drowning them, hanging them upside down and condemning them to eternal torture.

Gods were divided into different categories, often to do with the natural world. They were frequently associated with a particular theme: Ares with war, Pan with shepherds, Poseidon with the sea and Hades with the Underworld. Females, such as Athena (wisdom), Aphrodite (love and beauty) and Eris (strife) were also powerful and important. Their bodies took human form, but in a perfect,

Choose your favourite god in a Greek souvenir shop

divine way – they didn't get ill, injured or old. Gods and goddesses often fraternised with mortals, sometimes producing heroic offspring.

The grand finale of Greek mythology was the Trojan War, which pitted the Greeks against Troy. Zeus's daughter Helen, the most beautiful woman in the world, was married to Menelaus, who beat off competition from an array of suitors by promising Aphrodite he would sacrifice a hundred oxen. The wedding over, Menelaus neglected to make good his promise. When Paris, son of the king of Troy, fell in love with the married Helen, Aphrodite got revenge by helping Paris seduce and kidnap Helen. After much more to-ing and fro-ing, war broke out between the Greeks and Trojans, rumbling on for a decade, with the Greeks unable to penetrate Troy.

No victor emerged until another Greek king, Odysseus, came up with a cunning plan. The Greeks built a large wooden horse, filled it with soldiers, and left it close to the city gate, ostensibly as an offering to Athena. On finding the horse, the bemused Trojans dragged it into the town and debated what to do with it. Some wanted it burned, others to break it, and the less destructive (or suspicious) thought it should be given as an offering. Dissenters were dismissed and the horse was kept. The Trojans then set about celebrating the end of a decade of war. Once the natives were suitably drunk and sleepy, the Greeks emerged from the horse and laid waste to the city, raping, pillaging and murdering. So one of the most successful military strategies was accomplished.

THE IONIAN ISLANDS

This popular group of holiday islands lies off the west coast of Greece.

Corfu

Corfu's new port, Liman, receives cruise liners. It's quite a long way to get out of the terminal, and there will probably be one shuttle bus to the exit and then another one to the old town. The quickest route for walkers is the coast road, which will take about 15–30 minutes.

Although it's not the largest of the Ionian Islands (Kefalonia has that honour), Corfu is the most important and populous, and seems to be the most popular with cruise ships. Hot sun, beautiful beaches and the laidback lifestyle have been bringing in tourists for decades. Once under the protection of Venice, the island has retained its cultural connections with the Italian city, and elements of the architecture betray Venetian influence and style. Tourists from Italy are subsequently one of the main groups of visitors, though it is also popular with Brits (Britain also governed it at one time).

Corfu Town is to the east of the island, at the north end of a small peninsula. Its Italianate and Venetian architecture and three castles (the city is also known as Kastropolis – Fortress Town) earned it a place on the UNESCO World Heritage List in 2007. The city's labyrinthine cobblestone alleyways, many too narrow for cars to traverse, are aesthetically a delight to explore, although the ground surface can be uneven. Sadly the Italian influence seems to extend to the driving: look out for motorists taking a sneaky shortcut on the pavement (if there is one!).

Sights include the 16th-century **Church of Agios Spiridon**, Corfu's best-known place of worship. Its bell tower is the highest on the island. The inside is dense with ornamentation.

A silver display casket contains the remains of the eponymous St Spiridon; these are brought out four times a year and carried around the town. The saint is known as the Keeper of the City for having expelled the plague from Corfu. *St Spiridon. Tel: (26610) 39779. Open: 9am–2pm, but visits during Mass are discouraged. Free admission.*

The main museum here is the **Archaeological Museum**. The small

The bell tower of Agios Spiridon is easily seen from the busy streets of Corfu Town

Corfu has many fine beaches, such as this one at Agni, as well as little rocky coves

collection includes a Gorgon pediment from the Artemis temple (said to be Greece's oldest one), the Lion of Menecrates and a marble Apollo torso. *Vraili 5. Tel: (26610) 30680. Open: 8.30am–3pm. Admission charge.*

But most visitors to Kerkyra, to give Corfu its Greek name, will simply want to kick back on a fine beach, which are in plentiful supply. The island has 217km (135 miles) of coastline, including its capes. Many offer watersports, while others are more geared towards sunbathing and other leisurely pursuits.

Sitting over a drink or strolling are popular pastimes. Both can be done at Liston Arcade, a French-designed copy of the Rue de Rivoli in Paris. It has good views over a park, which explains why the prices are so much higher than elsewhere in Corfu. Just behind the arcade lies a tangle of narrow alleyways where much of the best shopping is to be done. Elegant Renaissance, Baroque and neoclassical architecture forms the backdrop to the retail activity.

348km (216 miles) southeast of Dubrovnik.

GERALD DURRELL'S CORFU

The island of Corfu became known to legions of schoolchildren, thanks to author and naturalist Gerald Durrell. Born to expatriate parents in India, he and his family came to the Ionian island in 1935. The ten-year-old Durrell soon developed an interest in the local fauna, and began to collect it with the help of a doctor, who told his young protégé: 'Here in Corfu, anything can happen.' The Durrells spent just five years on the island, returning to England at the outbreak of World War II. But Gerald's impressions and memories of both the island's natural life and his own family life were the inspiration for the classic *My Family and Other Animals* and two follow-up books. It was a fondly remembered time for the author, who wrote: 'My childhood in Corfu shaped my life. If I had the craft of Merlin, I would give every child the gift of my childhood.'

Kefalonia

Ships may either dock or anchor and tender here, depending on weather conditions and traffic. In either case, passengers are deposited right in the centre of Sámi.

Kefalonia (or Cephalonia, Cephallenia, Cephallonia or Kefallinia as it is variously spelled) is the largest of the Ionian Islands. It became widely known in 1993, when British author Louis de Bernières' bestselling novel *Captain Corelli's Mandolin* became the book that everybody was reading. A film adaptation, shot on the island, further raised Kefalonia's profile. Tourist numbers have since risen, although *Corelli* fans may be disappointed to find that the Venetian-style streets portrayed are no longer there, the result of the

Spectacular Smugglers Cove on Zante

1953 earthquake. As a result the towns, though not unpleasant, are a little bland in comparison with some other Greek islands. Despite the tourist influx, parts of the island, which has a relatively low population for its size, remain low-key and laid-back.

Kefalonia is not an easy island to travel around due to the mountainous territory and poor transport links, although Argostoli and Sámi, the island's main tourist hubs, are well linked. The former, also the capital, draws the bulk of the tourists, and has some excellent beaches in the vicinity.

163km (101 miles) southeast of Corfu.

Zante

Tenders are quite common at Zakynthos port, which is right beside the town.

A standard photo used to convey the brilliant blue sea, bright white sand and secluded beaches of the Greek islands is **Smugglers Cove** in Zante, a shock of white sand enclosed by a horseshoe of cliffs. The third Ionian island by size certainly has some postcard-perfect scenery. Those inspired by Zante's jaw-dropping beauty included Homer, who mentioned it in his epic poems, as well as Byron and Shelley. Needless to say the splendid beaches have not remained undiscovered: the island caters to high numbers of package tourists and can feel besieged in high season. One group here in high numbers are scuba divers, attracted by the variety of marine life

Dalmatian Coast, Greece and Turkey

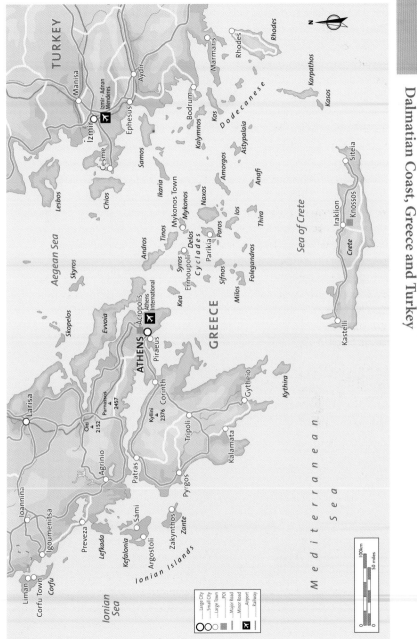

TURKEY

Manisa

Izmir-Adnan Menderes

Izmir

Çeşme

Ephesus

Aydin

Samos

Chios

Lesbos

Skyros

Aegean Sea

Skopelos

Larisa

Oiti 2152

Parnassos 2457

Agrinio

Ioannina

Igoumenitsa

Preveza

Liman

Corfu Town

Corfu

Ionian Sea

Lefkada

Kefalonia

Sami

Argostoli

Zakynthos

Zante

Ionian Islands

Patras

Kyllini 2376

Pyrgos

Tripoli

Kalamata

Corinth

ATHENS

Acropolis

Athens International

Piraeus

GREECE

Gytheio

Kythira

Tinos

Andros

Kea

Syros

Ermoupoli

Delos

Mykonos Town

Mykonos

Naxos

Paros

Parikia

Sifnos

Cyclades

Milos

Ios

Folegandros

Thira

Anafi

Amorgos

Astypalaia

Kos

Kalymnos

Bodrum

Marmaris

Rhodes

Rhodes

Dodecanese

Karpathos

Kasos

Sea of Crete

Iraklion

Knossos

Siteia

Crete

Kastelli

Mediterranean Sea

Ikaria

Large City

Small City

Large Town

POI

Major Road

Minor Road

Airport

Railway

100km

50 miles

0

0

and the caves suited to sub-aquatic exploration. The Bay of Laganas, celebrated for its clear, warm waters, boasts superb beaches. The Zante authorities perform a delicate balancing act between the travellers who want to visit them and the endangered loggerhead turtles that have been hatching their eggs there for the last 10,000 years.

The town of Zakynthos, also an alternative name for the whole island, has the Greek island staples: charming whitewashed houses, a plethora of boats and traditional tavernas. Stylistically it is Venetian, but like Kefalonia it suffered widespread damage in the earthquake of 1953 and has been significantly (and tastefully) rebuilt.

58km (36 miles) south of Kefalonia.

AEGEAN SEA

A Mediterranean bay that borders both Greece and Turkey, the Aegean Sea is home to the Greek capital plus a plethora of holiday islands.

Athens

From Piraeus, the port that serves Athens, the metro station is on the road that runs alongside the waterfront; simply exit the terminal and go left. Buses go along the same road if you don't fancy the walk, which can be around 20 minutes or so. Trains leave frequently and take less than half an hour.

Athens is one of the world's oldest cities, its history dating back over three millennia. Widely held to be the birthplace both of civilisation and democracy, it was once an unsurpassed

The Acropolis at sunset on an autumn day

centre of art and learning. Before being eclipsed by the Roman Empire, the city was the centre of the civilised world. Its heyday was during the Classical period of Ancient Greece, when the artefacts and constructions that define the country were created. The city subsequently entered a period of decline, although with the rise of the Byzantine Empire its fortunes took an upswing, and it did tolerably well throughout the Crusades. Athens emerged from a second slump, this time under the Ottomans, to become capital of the independent Greek state. Its modern-day status was consolidated with the successful hosting of the 2004 Olympics, nearly a century after the last time it hosted the Games that Greece gave to the world.

But, the Olympics aside, today Athens divides opinion. There are some who thrive on its heat, chaos and dishevelled charm. Others are thoroughly put off by the sheer enormity of the place, its pollution, traffic and concrete jungle vistas – block after block seemingly as far as the horizon. If you're in the latter category, you're likely to aim for the must-see sights rather than a comprehensive city tour.

Acropolis
The best known acropolis (high city) in the world, the buildings spread over the site mostly came into existence in the 5th century BC. The flagship structure is the **Parthenon**, the temple to Athena that has become a symbol of Ancient

Greece and its democracy. Its famous columns have been replicated ad infinitum. Technical aspects of the building are staggeringly advanced. In the pursuit of aesthetic perfection, optical refinements were made to counteract the effects of more prosaic adaptations such as curvature to deal with rainwater.

North of the Parthenon is the **Erechtheion**, famous for its **Porch of the Caryatids** (maidens), where the supporting pillars take the form of female figures. Both stand atop the hill around 150m (500ft) above sea level. From here, the true extent of Athens's urban sprawl becomes apparent. It is a gruelling climb, particularly in summer. Floor surfaces are often uneven, so wear appropriate footwear. Another downside is the scaffolding that surrounds the Parthenon as part of renovation works. While obviously intended to preserve the site for future generations, it can be something of a downer for your holiday snaps!

But despite the heat, the climb, the scaffolding and the crowds, the Acropolis is a must-see. It contains nearly two dozen sights of note, including gates, statues, temples, theatres and sanctuaries.
Acropolis Hill, Plaka. Tel: (210) 321 4172. Open: Apr–Oct 8am–sunset; Nov–Mar 8am–2.30pm. Admission charge, which includes all Unification of Archaeological Sites. Metro: Acropolis.

Walk: Athens

The size of Athens and the heat and pollution mean that it's not the ideal walking city. Nevertheless, its frenetic atmosphere appeals to some, and does have a certain quintessential Greekness about it. The following is a suggested route for those who want to see more than the most obvious attractions.

Take the metro (or a taxi) to Syntagma.

1 Plateia Syntagma

The heart of modern-day Athens, the Bavarian-designed Constitution Square came into being in 1834 to reflect the city's newly acquired capital status. There is plenty to see, including the Parliament building, National Gardens and Tomb of the Unknown Soldier. The top of the hour sees the changing of the wonderfully attired *evzones* (the elite unit of presidential guards).
Take the street running west, immediately opposite Parliament, Ermou. Offsetting the neoclassical buildings that house the shops are various quirky street performers.

2 Panaghia Kapnikarea

This small, pretty Byzantine church, dating from around the 11th century, was built on the site of an ancient Greek temple.
Open: Sat–Mon & Wed 8am–2pm, Tue, Thur & Fri 4.30–9.30pm.
Turn left off Ermou, and take the next left along Mitropleos to the cathedral.

3 Megali Mitropoli

Athens's largest church hosts royal coronations plus the weddings and funerals of the city's great and good.
Tel: (210) 322 1308. Open: daily 7am–7pm (may close in the afternoon). To the left as you leave is the next church.

4 Mikri Mitropoli

The fascinating Byzantine Church of Agios Eleftherios, or 'little cathedral' as it is known, includes marble from the Ancient Agora and carved reliefs depicting ancient Athenian festivals.
Tel: (210) 322 1308. Open: daily 7am–7pm.
Turn right down Agia Filotheis until you reach the pedestrianised Adrianou. Continue uphill to a small square with a church.

5 Agia Ekaterini

The square that hosts this 18th-century church also contains some excavations.
Opening hours vary.
Turn right past the church.

6 Choragic Monument of Lysicrates

Built in 334 BC, this marble monument is the sole survivor of a series built to commemorate award-winning concerts and plays. Venture forward a little and you'll have a view of the Arch of Hadrian.

Walk away from the arch along Epimenidou, up some steps then turn right onto Stratonos. Stay on the same road, circumventing the Acropolis, then turn right up Klepsydras.

7 The Roman Forum

Despite living in the shadow of its Greek predecessor, its Tower of the Winds, an octagonal marble structure adorned with wind deities, built in the 1st century BC is well worth a look.

Tel: (210) 324 5220. Open: May–Oct 8am–7pm; Nov–Apr 8am–3pm. Admission charge, either separately or including all Unification of Archaeological Sites.
Go north along Eolou, turn left into Pandrosou which brings you to a square, Plateia Monastiraki.

8 Plateia Monastiraki

A mosque, turned jail, turned Museum of Greek Folk Art, plus a flea market to the west are in or by the square, or you could head to the Ancient Agora or Acropolis. Alternatively, seek out one of the nearby restaurants and relax.
It is one stop on the metro from Plateia Monastiraki back to Plateia Syntagma.

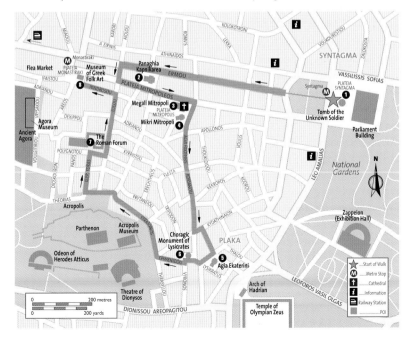

THE OLYMPIC GAMES

Like much about Ancient Greece, the Olympics are shrouded in myth. One legend goes that Heracles, son of Zeus, initiated the spectacle, building the stadium after completing his 12 labours, and his 400 paces established the track length. The first games are believed to have taken place in 776 BC. Religious sacrifices and ceremonies for Zeus alternated with the sport, while winners were venerated through poetry and statues. Participants – young men – competed in the nude. The rise of Roman power sent the Games into decline, and they were finally outlawed as a pagan festival in AD 393. It was to be over 1,500 years before the first Modern Olympic Games revived the phenomenon.

Ancient Agora

Once the heart and soul of Athens' social, political and civic life, this site (*agora* means 'place of assembly') was the city marketplace, with schools, theatres, homes, shops and market stalls all contributing to the buzz. Here Athenians would once have heard Socrates opine away on the state of the world, before he was executed for 'introducing strange gods and corrupting youth'. St Paul also attracted the ire of the locals, whom he labelled superstitious. Today the site feels a little desolate, but there is enough here to help you mentally piece together how it might have been.

Adrianou 24, Monastiraki.
Tel: (210) 321 0185. Open: summer
8am–7.30pm; winter 8am–3pm.
Admission charge, either separately or
including all Unification of
Archaeological Sites. Metro: Thiseio.

National Archaeological Museum

Greece's most important museum is home to some of the most significant art and archaeological finds from prehistory to late antiquity. The Mask of Agamemnon (a funeral mask which historians believe in fact predates the legendary Greek king; nonetheless the name remains), the Marathon Boy sculpture and depictions of various Greek gods are among the abundance of highlights. Unlike many of Athens's wonders, the museum is fully wheelchair accessible.

Patission 44, Omonia. Tel: (210) 821 7717.
Open: summer Tue–Sun 8am–7pm,
Mon 1pm–7pm; winter Tue–Sun
8.30am–3pm, Mon 1pm–7pm.
Admission charge. Metro: Viktoria.

One of the pretty streets in Parikia, Paros

The Cyclades
Paros

As is the case on most of the Greek islands, the port, which is often relatively busy, is an easy walk to town.

Picture-perfect Paros gets much less attention than its fellow Cycladic isle of Mykonos – which is all the better for the lucky visitors able to wander its streets in relative calm and quiet. Make sure to take your sunglasses – the whitewashed buildings give off a dazzling glare. If the island is famous for something, it continues the bright white theme: the marble from which the Venus de Milo was fashioned came from here. (Paros's marble has even made it into the dictionary through the term Parian, referring to the marble, or a fine, unglazed porcelain resembling it.)

The capital is **Parikia**, although it is so serene and near silent in places, that the word 'capital' seems inappropriate. The absence of cars throughout much of the town adds to the calm. Late afternoon is particularly somnolent, with many businesses closed for a siesta. This is a wonderful time to head for the back streets and enjoy the authentic Greece. Houses here are styled in the typically Cycladic way: whitewashed walls supporting flat roofs, with navy blue doors and window frames.

But while daytime Paros is sleepy, at night the capital is a retail hub. And the merchandise reflects the town's tourist appeal: high-end designer

The beautiful pulpit of Ekatontapiliani Church in Parikia

boutiques and fashion outlets line the passageways, interspersed with pleasant cafés and restaurants. Strolling is the thing here; there are few landmarks. A notable exception is the **Ekatontapiliani Church** (*open: 7am–9pm*), famed for its striking interior. The name translates as the Church of a Hundred Gates. Legend has it that only 99 of the said gates have been found, and when the hundredth is opened, Constantinople will be reunited with Greece.

160km (100 miles) southeast of Athens.

Mykonos

Mykonos's windmills grace the coast on your approach. Ships dock at Tourlos, 2km (1¼ miles) from Mykonos Town. A shuttle bus will be laid on. The walk is on a pavementless road along which coaches hurtle, and it is not advised.

Costly, cosmopolitan and with a thriving nightlife, Mykonos is the *grande dame* of the Cyclades' tourist scene. The 'Ibiza of the Cyclades' might be pushing it somewhat, but if you want late-night revelry, the island will oblige. The diverse entertainment options include a flourishing gay scene, earning Mykonos the appellation 'the gay capital of the Aegean'. Ships here often dock late into the night or until early the next morning, so cruise passengers can let their hair down.

Island and main town share the same name, and for that reason you will often hear the latter referred to as **Chora**, or 'the town'. Most of the activity is centred here (the exception being some superb beaches towards the south). Those who do leave the town usually do so to sail to **Delos**, a central Cycladic island boasting a plethora of historical finds. Mykonos itself has the same staples that make the Cyclades so attractive – meandering alleys, whitewashed houses and impossibly bright pink flowers spilling down from balconies and staircases.

The island's beaches are particularly pretty. Super Paradise attracts gay and nude bathers, while Paradise attracts a younger crowd. Agrari and Elia are also popular with gay travellers, and the latter offers water-skiing, parasailing and windsurfing. Platis Gialos, which is within easy reach of Mykonos Town, is popular and packed, while the nearby Psarou draws in the beautiful people.

Mykonos and other islands of the Cyclades beyond

A street scene in Ermoupoli, the capital of Syros

Plenty of other stretches of sand run the gamut from party beach to serene. Shopping and dining options are good but expensive.

Though the large numbers of tourists may detract from the Greek island ambience a little, there is one visitor who always delights: Petros the Pelican has been the island mascot for half a century. The first bearer of the name (a wounded bird who was adopted by the townsfolk after a local fisherman nursed him back from injury) is sadly no more, but you might see one of the three pelicans, including Petros II, who succeeded the original.

153km (95 miles) southeast of Athens.

Syros
Picturesque white buildings clutter the hillside on the Syros approach. Ships dock centrally.

Though not as prominent on the tourist circuit as some of the other Cyclades islands, Syros itself has the atmosphere of a larger town. This is owing, in part, to its history as the country's leading commercial and industrial hub. It was also Greece's main port, before being surpassed by Piraeus in the 19th century. But Syros's administrative status has not totally dissipated: capital Ermoupoli is also the capital of the entire archipelago.

There's a handful of sizeable churches to visit, and Ermoupoli's hillside location affords great views for those prepared to climb. If you've had your fill of perfect tourist beaches, the small promenade slightly to the north of the port is a lovely spot to sit and watch local families and fishermen go about their leisure and business respectively.

120km (75 miles) southeast of Athens.

Dalmatian Coast, Greece and Turkey

TURKEY
Istanbul

From the port at Karakoy, it's a 45-minute walk to Sultanahmet, where the main sites are based. Taxis, which usually offer good value, take ten minutes.

The only city to straddle two continents, Istanbul is a fascinating blend of west and east. In some ways, by cruise is not the best way to see the Turkish capital: the city is so large and engaging that a day or two is simply not enough. But the major sights are concentrated in a relatively small area, and your time in the port will whet your appetite for a return.

It is not only geographically that Europe's largest city is so sizeable;

Istanbul's history is similarly extensive. It stretches back some 3,000 years, during which time the metropolis went from Byzantium to Constantinople to Istanbul (as observed in the famous swing song) and served as capital of various empires from the Roman to the Ottoman.

Istanbul's character and history are nicely encapsulated in its main attractions. This is a city of constant activity and trade (on show in the Grand Bazaar), and a one-time battleground of major religions (see the basilica-turned-mosque-turned-museum of Aya Sofya). A cityscape of minarets and soundtrack of frequent calls to prayer would normally seem to fit incongruously with the Western brand names on sale – but in Istanbul it

seems to work. In a city literally and metaphorically divided in two by the Bosphorus River, most of the sights are on the European side, which is where you are likely to spend most if not all of your time on a short visit. Wherever you are, there will be a sense of things (often commercial) happening. Istanbul is a place of great hospitality.

Aya Sofya

The huge dome of Aya Sofya is the distinctive feature that has led to the former church's status as the embodiment of Byzantine architecture. Constructed in the 6th century at the behest of Byzantine Emperor Justinian, the basilica spent a millennium as the centre of the Eastern Orthodox Church. When Constantinople fell to the Turks, Sultan Mehmed II had it converted into a mosque. Out went the Christian bells, altar, iconostasis and sacrificial paraphernalia; in their stead came the mihrab, minbar and minarets. In its five centuries as Istanbul's main mosque, it served as inspiration for various replicas. As of 1935, it has been a museum. Beyond the sheer impressiveness of its size, there are many fabulous mosaics on show.
Sultanahmet. Open: summer Tue–Sun 9am–6pm; winter Tue–Sun 9am–4.30pm. Closed: Mon. Admission charge.

Blue Mosque

Named for the colour of its internal walls, the Blue Mosque is one of the

The Blue Mosque of Istanbul dates from the early 17th century

Dalmatian Coast, Greece and Turkey

city's top attractions and a landmark on its skyline. Now four centuries old, the Sultan Ahmed Mosque, to use its official but seldom-heard name, is one of only two mosques in Turkey to have six minarets. The distinctive roof is completed by a series of domes and half-domes. Inside, the mosque is divided into two parts: a large front section for worshippers and a busier back section for tourists. The buzz made by the latter means that it does not really feel like a place of worship. Nonetheless, the spectacular interior of the domes, plus the interplay of the windows and lights, certainly repay a visit.
Sultanahmet. Open: 8.30am–10.30pm except prayer times. Free admission, but donation appreciated.

Kapalıçarşı (Grand Bazaar)

A tourist attraction as much as a retail outlet, Istanbul's Kapalıçarşı, better known as the Grand Bazaar, is a wonderful collision of Western capitalism and Eastern traditions. One of the world's largest covered markets, the labyrinthine shopping centre attracts upwards of 250,000 visitors daily to its 58 streets and 6,000 shops. The narrow, domed walkways are teeming with shoppers, traders and boys weaving through them carrying small glasses of tea balanced precariously on trays.

Beyazit. www.kapalicarsi.org.tr (website in Turkish). Open: Mon–Sat 8am–7.30pm. Closed: Sun. Tram: Beyazit.

Locals enjoying shisha pipes in an Istanbul square

Topkapı Palace

The seat of power for the Ottoman sultans for 400 years, this place is as opulent and indulgent as you would expect. An incredible 5,000 people, from sultans and concubines to eunuchs and slaves, lived within the palace. From the meeting rooms to the harem, the place is dripping with medieval bling.

Gulhane Park, near Sultanahmet. Tel: (212) 512 0480. www.topkapisarayi.gov.tr. Open: summer Wed–Mon 9am–6pm; winter Wed–Mon 9am–4pm. Closed: Tue. Admission charge.

568km (353 miles) northeast of Athens.

Ephesus

Ephesus is usually visited on a day trip from Kusadasi. Taxis are relatively inexpensive, and usually work out better value than the ship's organised tour.

It has nowhere near the celebrity of Athens, but the ancient Turkish city of Ephesus is a wonderful site, and was even the capital of Asia in Roman times. For visitors, its lower profile is a boon; rather than traipsing around en masse, you might get some sections of the place almost to yourself. If you're lucky enough to be in this situation (for which you'd probably need to come out of season), the atmosphere will be marvellous. You can imagine St Paul sermonising (before he was booted out by the Ephesian silversmiths for saying

THE SEVEN SLEEPERS

The myth of the Seven Sleepers of Ephesus appears in both the Roman Martyrology and the Qu'ran. It centres on seven young men who were accused of being Christians. Rather than meeting the grisly end meted out to others, the men were given some time to recant. But they didn't; instead they gave away their possessions to the poor and climbed up a mountain to pray together in a cave. Once there, they fell asleep, and the irate emperor had the mouth of the cave sealed. A few decades later, the landowner reopened the cave. Rather than skeletons, he found the seven young men, who awoke, believing they had only been sleeping for a day. One returned to Ephesus, where he was staggered to see crosses attached to the buildings. After telling their incredible story to a bishop, the seven sleepers died, praising God.

that their Diana models were not divine). The various points of interest are spread out over a wide area. While much still remains to be excavated, what there is gives a telling impression of Ephesus's erstwhile grandeur.

Once again, the Ancient Greeks' love of drama is evident. There are two theatres on show, the main one of which is a 24,000-seater venue, thought to be the largest outdoor theatre in the ancient world. The latter is particularly impressive to behold, and you can even pass through the tunnel that led from the exterior to the arena, imagining yourself to be a gladiator or suchlike. Other highlights include the Temple of Hadrian, the Celsius Library and the Marble Way (where Ephesus's wealthier individuals resided).

Open: summer 8.30am–7pm; winter 8am–5pm. Admission charge.

380km (236 miles) south of Istanbul.

Dalmatian Coast, Greece and Turkey

The Great Theatre at Ephesus was constructed during the 3rd century BC

Bodrum Castle now contains the fascinating Underwater Archaeology Museum

Bodrum

Look out for Bodrum Castle as you enter the town's attractive bay. Ships usually tender passengers to land (some dock) at Bodrum. The town is within easy reach but be prepared for a climb. Taxis wait around the cruise port area.

Once a fishing village, for the time being Bodrum seems to have avoided the seemingly inevitable trajectory from sleepy hamlet to ghastly tourist trap. That's not to say it's not touristy – it is. But the town has not yet been blighted by the ugly development that has scarred some Turkish resorts (although the pine hills behind it are home to increasing numbers of villas). It also still has a sprinkling of cultural attractions. As well as tourists, the southwest Aegean port also draws in a high number of yachts, which can be seen along the marina, and artistic types.

The ideal time to go is outside peak season, thus avoiding the tourist hordes. The main sight is **Bodrum Kalesi** (Bodrum Castle) also known as the Castle of St Peter, which contains the city's **Underwater Archaeology Museum**. Standing sentinel in a prominent position on the coast, the castle dates from the 15th century. It now makes for a highly enjoyable tourist attraction, with some splendid exhibits, many of which were salvaged from ancient shipwrecks lying at the bottom of the Aegean Sea. As well as various artefacts, some of which make the castle itself look relatively new by comparison, there are delicate models and pleasant artwork, and a few peacocks strutting around outside. The castle also affords extensive and beautiful bay views.
Southeast of Bodrum marina. Tel: (252) 316 2516. www.bodrum-museum.com. Open: Tue–Sat 9am–noon & 2–7pm. Admission charge.

Close to the castle, the mosque and mausoleum are the other main landmarks. The curved harbour is buzzing with activity both nautical and culinary: yachts one side and restaurants and shops on the other. It makes for a lively place for a promenade, but for a beach you need to leave the town proper.

92km (57 miles) south of Ephesus.

Marmaris

Marmaris's picturesque bay is often more lauded than the town itself. Liners either anchor or dock at the port's ferry terminal. The old town is a short walk across the square.

A victim of untrammelled development, Marmaris is likely to be too touristy for many travellers' tastes. But though a week's or fortnight's package deal here might be rather dispiriting, on a cruise a one-night stop to experience the port's thriving party scene can be a welcome change from the worthier sightseeing you might have done elsewhere. That is not to paint Marmaris as a culture-free zone. Its castle, though not in the same league

Dalmatian Coast, Greece and Turkey

The harbour at Marmaris

as Bodrum's, is well positioned for enjoying bay vistas.

If the town itself really leaves you cold, there are several potential excursions, depending on how long your ship is in port. With a high-speed boat, you can be in Rhodes in less than an hour. The village of Turunc, 20km (12½ miles) south of Marmaris, is another pleasant boat trip away. A 12km (8-mile) minibus ride followed by short hop by boat brings you to Cleopatra's Island, whose fine sands and aquamarine waters are top-notch, even by Turkish standards. It is a bumpy yet panoramic bus ride to Datça, a former pirates' enclave. As pretty as Marmaris, it is far quieter.

78km (48 miles) east of Bodrum.

Antalya

From afar, the most prominent feature of the coastline near Antalya is its old castle. Larger vessels tender guests to the Roman harbour, while smaller ones dock. The sights are all close at hand.

The place Atatürk is said to have described as 'without doubt the most beautiful place in the world', Antalya is another package-holiday favourite. Despite its many remains, it has a more modern feel than many history-steeped coastal resorts. Its cliff-top location, surrounded by mountains, adds to the resort's charm. The action centres on Kaleçi. Antalya's historical centre is now devoted to tourism, and is packed with places for visitors to eat, sleep, party and generally spend their cash. Its Ottoman character has been preserved through restoration. Amidst the tourist trappings you'll find a mosque, with its Yivli Minare (fluted minaret), which today houses an ethnographic exhibition.

Nearby is the **Antalya Müzesi** (Antalya Museum), one of Turkey's most important museums. It consists of 13 exhibition halls and an outdoor gallery, hosting a cornucopia of finds including mosaics, coins, statues, art and children's toys.
Cumhuriyet Caddesi. Open: Tue–Sun 9am–6pm. Closed: Mon. Admission charge.

216km (134 miles) east of Marmaris.

THE DODECANESE
Also in the Aegean Sea, these islands lie off Turkey's southwest coast.

Kalymnos
Kalymnos's hills make a pleasant panorama on your entry to the port. The town centre is immediately obvious.

The limestone cliffs, caves and overhangs of Kalymnos not only serve to beautify the Aegean island, but have made it popular among rock climbers. Aside from its craggy appeal, the island has much in common with the rest of the Dodecanese and wider Greek

Antalya is an ancient city as well as a modern tourist resort

islands: Italianate architecture, brilliant white buildings with blue trimmings and the lazy comings and goings of various vessels. Pothia is the capital and main port. Its waterfront is full of restaurants and cafés with outside seating, and one pleasure is to stroll along it or get a drink and watch the traffic. Those prepared to climb the town's hills are rewarded with some agreeable views of the bay. Top of the attractions (literally – it's right at the peak) is the **Monastery of Saint Sava**, whose pretty russet domes crown the town nicely. If you can't face the hot climb, take a bus or a cab towards Vilhadia. The monastery is joined in its lofty position by another church.
Monastery. On the road to Vilhadia. Open: approx 10am–7pm. Free admission.

41km (25 miles) southwest of Bodrum.

Kos

The ascending Italianate buildings will catch your eye on the approach to Kos's port. The town centre is a short walk away.

The island whose gift to the world was Hippocrates, the father of medicine, is now a temple to tourism. Late at night, it sometimes seems that, were it not for the weather, you could be in any large English city centre on a Friday night. If this is not your cup of tea, you may wish to avoid Bar Street. Shops stay open late to cater to both the party crowd and the more sedate cruisers heading back to their ship after a meal. And the pretty beaches are often awash with tourists sleeping off the excesses of the night before.

But there's more to Kos than holiday hedonism. The main town, also called Kos, boasts some fine Italianate

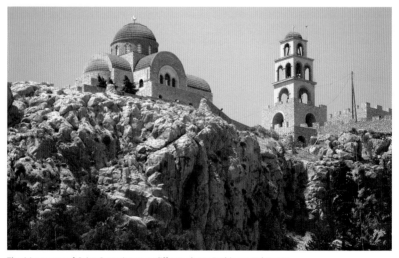

The Monastery of Saint Sava sits on a cliff top above Pothia on Kalymnos

A view over Kos Town

architecture, which makes an interesting contrast with the minarets of its Turkish quarter. (Though part of Greece, Kos is far closer to the Turkish mainland, which is evident in the feel of the place.) A Roman forum, 18th-century mosque and **Archaeological Museum** are among the more cerebral ways to pass the time.

Archaeological Museum. Plateia Eleftherios. Open: 8am–2.30pm. Admission charge.

20km (12¹/₂ miles) southeast of Bodrum.

Rhodes

Depending on the size of your ship, it will dock either at the Commercial Port, east of the old centre, or the nearer Mandraki Harbour. Neither is too long a walk.

Boasting one of the largest medieval towns in Europe, Rhodes attracts the lion's share of visitors to the Dodecanese. The old town is in Rhodes City, the island's capital and port. Delightful cobbled alleyways and myriad pretty buildings reflect the place's old alternating rulers (Turkish and Italian). The town's layout similarly embodies its ethnic influences, divided as it is into the Knights, Turkish and Jewish quarters. Though some of the less welcome accoutrements of the holiday industry are present (if it's tourist tat or fast food you're after, you won't have to walk far), Rhodes City remains eye-catching enough to qualify as a UNESCO World Heritage Site. Sadly, its contribution to the Seven Wonders of the Ancient World, the Colossus of Rhodes (a huge statue of the Greek gold Helios), is long gone.

There's still plenty to see for those of a historical leaning. Amble down the Odós Ippoton (Avenue of the Knights), as grand a thoroughfare as its name implies. **The Palace of the Knights** is one of many imposing medieval buildings on the street. It had the dubious honour of being restored as a holiday home for fascist leader Mussolini (his name appears on a plaque by the entrance). He was executed before he could take advantage of the property.

Open: Mon 12.30–7pm, Tue–Sun 8am–7pm. Admission charge.

Another knightly building, the old hospital, now houses the **Archaeology Museum**. Highlights include statues of the Aphrodite of Rhodes and the Aphrodite of Thalassia. For a

The grand entrance of the Palace of the Knights in Rhodes City

quintessentially Turkish experience, try the **Municipal Baths**.

Archaeology Museum. Plateia Argykastrou. Tel: (241) 027 657. Open: Tue–Sun 8.30am–7pm. Closed: Mon. Admission charge. Municipal Baths. Plateia Arionos. Open: Tue–Sat 11am–7pm. Closed: Sun & Mon. Admission charge.

110km (68 miles) southeast of Bodrum.

CRETE

The stately Venetian fortress at the entrance to Heraklion's port stands as an impressive legacy of Crete's time under the Republic of Venice. From the port gates, go right along the waterfront, then left along Odos 25 Avgoustou to reach the town centre. Taxis are also on standby at the port.

Greece's largest island (and the Med's fifth) is also one of its most popular holiday destinations, with 15 per cent of the country's visitors arriving at Iraklion. The Cretan capital, and the main port, is situated on the north coast of the island, which is also home to the main tourist hubs. The west coast and villages offer less developed and less crowded options. The fourth largest city in Greece, Iraklion has a different feel from the usual sleepy ports that cruise ships frequent in the region. With its own version of the Greek language, and distinct culture and traditions, Crete sets itself apart from the mainland. Yet it holds an important place in the country's mythology: in Greek legend, the island was the birthplace of Zeus.

Cruise passengers will first find themselves in Plateia Venizelou, a popular city square with Venetian echoes. Filled with shops, it is home to the **Morosini Fountain**, whose jets of water emanate from lions' mouths, and

The port at Iraklion, Crete

Agios Markos, a 13th-century basilica (*opening hours vary; free admission*). The **Archaeological Museum** is the town's top attraction. One of Greece's best museums, it contains the world's greatest collection of Minoan art. An extensive array of exhibits, from fertility symbols, rhytons, weapons, jewellery and frescoes, paints a detailed portrait of the Bronze Age Minoan civilisation. A more limited range is on display while the museum undergoes modernisation and expansion. It is due to reopen in 2010.

Part of the reconstructed palace at Knossos, Crete

Xanthoudidou 2. Tel: (821) 022 4630. Open: Apr–Oct Mon 1–7.30pm, Tue–Fri 8am–7.30pm; Nov–Mar Mon noon–5pm, Tue–Sun 8.30am–3pm. Admission charge.

Iraklion is too busy for some visitors' tastes. A popular excursion is to **Knossos**, 5km (3 miles) south of the capital. This ancient centre of Minoan culture, rediscovered at the end of the 19th century, has been extensively restored to resemble the town as it would have looked, replete with palace, throne room, apartments, baths, frescoes and so on. While some shudder at the impudence, others find it provides a better glimpse of Minoan civilisation than would a bunch of old ruins. The site can easily absorb a day. *Open: Mon–Sat 8am–5pm. Admission charge. Bus: 2 from station A.*

344km (214 miles) south of Athens.

CYPRUS

From Limassol, you'll be walking upwards of 20 minutes (turn right when you leave the port) to the old town. A shuttle is usually laid on for the 3km (2-mile) journey. The centre of Larnaca is much nearer to the port, just over the road, but buses still make the journey.

The third largest Mediterranean island is a hugely popular tourist destination, despite the political strife that means the northern part is controlled by Turkey. Cyprus's location, quite far south in Mediterranean terms, and close to Greece, Turkey, the Middle East

The beach at Agia Napa near Larnaca, Cyprus

and Egypt, makes it a popular port on winter cruises as well as those during the more clement months. Two mountain ranges give the island geographical diversity (as well as offering hiking and winter skiing). There is plenty by way of historical architecture, with Greek and Roman ruins, monasteries and castles punctuating the territory, much of which is happily unspoilt by the excesses of tourism.

Two ports accommodate cruise ships, **Limassol**, to the south of the island, and **Larnaca**, which lies further east. The main port, Limassol, also known as Lemesos, has a pleasant old town and a less pleasant new town. Attractions include a medieval castle, which houses the **Cyprus Medieval Museum**.
Near the Old Port. Tel: (25) 305 419.
Open: Mon–Sat 9am–between
5 and 7.30pm, depending on the
season; Sun 10am–1pm.
Admission charge.

Smaller Larnaca also has a fort and Turkish district of interest. It is used as a gateway to **Agia Napa** in the southeast. There are a wealth of watersports on offer at this resort, whose beaches have earned the Blue Flag for their cleanliness, but its renown is as a nightlife centre. Grime, house and garage are currently popular in Agia Napa's clubs.

485km (300 miles) east of Rhodes.

The south

Though many Mediterranean cruises will feature predominantly European ports, a stop in the south of the region can make a colourful juxtaposition. While some cruise lines factor in a non-EU country purely to be able to offer their passengers duty-free shopping, there is much more to be gained by a day south of the Med than simply reduced-price merchandise.

One obvious plus is the weather. The few extra notches on the thermometer are a boon in winter, allowing liners to continue to ply the Mediterranean over Christmas and the New Year. But more than that, the southern countries offer a different cultural experience. Their predominantly Islamic societies lend the North African nations a contrasting style of architecture, music, dress, diet, attitude and interaction. Leaving the European 'comfort zone' can therefore be an enlightening excursion. And the cruise set-up – transport to and from the destination, and a limited time there – is the ideal way to explore what for many passengers might be uncharted territory.

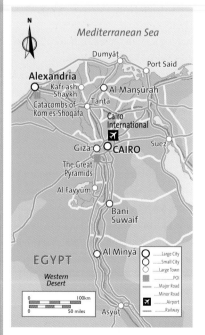

EGYPT
Alexandria

Alexandria's port is fairly central, with the Corniche just a 20-minute walk away. However, the town is so long (spreading out over 32km/20 miles down the coast) that you may prefer to take a taxi to your particular destination. You'll easily find one at the port, but be sure to establish the fare in advance.

Named after, and built at the behest of Alexander the Great, Egypt's second city was once second only to Rome in terms of learning and trade. Famous for both the largest library in the world and as home to one of the Seven Wonders of the Ancient World (the Lighthouse of Alexandria), it was also the court of Cleopatra. Though much of its glory is no more, the city retains several archaeological sites and noteworthy buildings.

History is likely to top most visitors' to-do lists in Alexandria. The bizarrely brilliant **Catacombs of Kom es-Shoqafa** are Roman-era burial chambers, decorated with extraordinary reliefs drawing on mythology.
Shari Mansura. Open: 9am–5pm, Ramadan 9am–3pm. Admission charge.

The **Graeco-Roman Museum**, which has been in operation for over a century, provides an excellent introduction to Alexandria's classical past. At the time of publication it was closed for renovation, so phone ahead before planning a visit. In any case, it's worth viewing the building from the outside.

Inside the Catacombs of Kom es-Shoqafa in Alexandria

THE LIBRARY OF ALEXANDRIA

Founded by one of the Ptolemies at the start of the 3rd century BC, the illustrious Library of Alexandria featured gardens, plus rooms for eating, reading, meetings and lectures (a prototype of today's universities). The books of the time were papyrus productions, and readers could take solace from the inscription on the wall that described it as: 'The place of the cure of the soul.' Royal-funded buyers kept stocks up to date by scouring the fairs of Rhodes and Athens, and it is said that books were removed from every ship that docked in Alexandria, with copies returned in their stead. The precise destruction of the library, which occurred sometime before the 2nd century AD, has not been definitively established, with Julius Caesar, Aurelian, Theophilus and the Muslim Conquest all potentially responsible.

Mathaf El Romani Street, Downtown. Tel: (3) 486 5820; www.grm.gov.eg. Open: 9am–5pm or 4pm during Ramadan. Closed: Fri 11.30am–1.30pm. Admission charge.

For a retail experience, the city's **souk** (bazaar), a block from the seafront, will be a novelty for anyone unused to Eastern bartering cultures. You can pick up everything from herbs to rugs.

180km (112 miles) northwest of Cairo.

Giza

Despite its many attractions and its importance, cruise passengers on a short stopover will often bypass Alexandria in favour of the Egypt's legendary pyramids in Giza. It's a longer journey than the average

(Cont. on p122)

Walk: Alexandria

Though Alexandria is a sprawling metropolis, many of its sights are within fairly easy reach of each other. This walk takes in a selection of the main attractions, from the old to the new. The route brings you back to the waterfront so you can round off the day with dinner or a drink overlooking the sea, then head back to the boat.

Leave at least half a day, though if you linger it's more likely to take a whole one.

Start at the easternmost point of the Eastern Harbour. To the east is the library.

1 Bibliotheca Alexandrina (Alexandria Library)

A striking counterpoint to the ancient library as was, this Norwegian-designed contemporary building is quite spectacular. It was opened in 2002 and has room for around eight million books.
Tel: (3) 483 9999. www.bibalex.org.
Open: Sat–Thur 11am–7pm, Fri 3–7pm.
Admission charge.
Go southwest along the promenade.

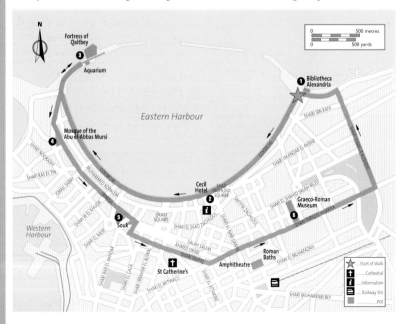

The Fortress of Qaitbey stands over the Eastern Harbour

2 The Corniche

The Corniche is Alexandria's 2km (1¼-mile) seafront area and is home to graceful 19th-century buildings. Halfway along, the **Cecil Hotel** once accommodated Winston Churchill. *Cecil Hotel. 16 Saad Zaghloul Square. Tel: (3) 487 7173. www.sofitel.com. Keep walking to the end of the road. You'll see the fortress up ahead.*

3 Fortress of Qaitbey

Incorporating some of the huge blocks that once formed part of Alexandria's renowned lighthouse, this castle dates from much later, at five centuries old. *Tel: (3) 486 5106. Open: summer 9am–6pm; winter 9am–4pm. Admission charge. Turn back the way you've come, but instead of going along the Corniche, take the right fork when the road divides. The mosque will be on your right.*

4 Mosque of the Abu el-Abbas Mursi

This mosque is exceptionally beautiful and at 'only' two centuries old is relatively modern. The soaring minaret stands at 73m (240ft). Spend some time on the lively square next to the mosque. *Opening hours vary. Closed to women. Keep walking for about 1km (²/₃ mile), then turn right towards the market.*

5 Souk

Pick up a souvenir of Egypt from the vivid souk, or simply enjoy the bustle. *Continue in the same direction, taking any of the parallel streets going southeast onto Shari Taufiq or Salah Salem. Walk to the end and turn left onto Shari Tariq el Hurriya. Continue to the museum.*

6 Graeco-Roman Museum

Even if this excellent collection is still closed for renovation when you visit, its Greek-style building is nonetheless worthy of a photo. *Go back towards the sea and rejoin the Corniche. Finish off the day with dinner or a drink at one of the many restaurants and cafés along the waterfront. You could even try a traditional shisha! Relax and watch couples promenading and children playing. If it's the right time of day, you are well positioned to watch the sun go down before returning to the ship.*

excursion, but the fact that the pyramids are the only one of the Seven Wonders of the Ancient World remaining persuades many visitors to make the 180km (112-mile) trip from the port. The Great Pyramids complex comprises three main pyramids, several satellite structures and the Great Sphinx. Dating from the 26th century BC, the pyramids were built as tombs for kings. In total, there are nearly a hundred spread out through the desert. Though every visitor will be familiar with the structures from film and photographs, viewing them up close and pondering the incredible dimensions and feats of engineering involved is quite something else.
Open: daily 8am–4 or 5pm.
Admission charge.

A trip to the pyramids can also take in Cairo, the bustling Egyptian capital. The City of a Thousand Minarets, whose origins are in Roman times, has a rich, pan-religious architectural inheritance of mosques, churches and synagogues.

MALTA
Valletta

Valletta's orderliness, offset by the cliffs of the Maltese coastline, makes the approach a particularly pretty one. From the port it's about a 15-minute uphill walk into town, or you may prefer a taxi as fares are reasonable. There is no need to buy a ticket for a cab before you exit through the gates, despite what port officials might try to persuade you!

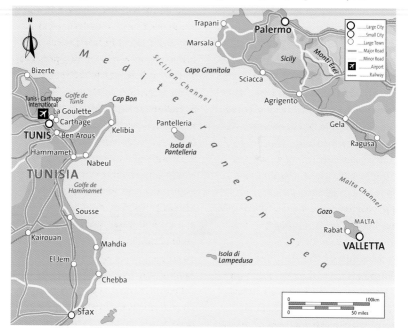

Inside the Grand Master's Palace, Valletta

Malta's geographical smallness is not representative of its strategic importance in history. The islands' location, close to the small stretch of water between Sicily and Tunisia through which all vessels going from west to east or vice versa had to pass, made it of great interest to past civilisations. The archipelago was controlled, at times, by the Phoenicians, Arabs, Sicilians, Normans and British, among others. This has bequeathed Malta an identity that is at once a hotchpotch of international influences and strongly Maltese. The country is probably most closely associated with the Knights of St John, the Christian Order who founded Valletta.

Something of the courtly still surrounds the Maltese capital in the 21st century. Known as the city built 'by gentlemen, for gentlemen', the walled city of Valletta is renowned for its architectural quality. As you'd expect from Malta's diverse history, there is an array of styles evident. Renaissance and Baroque influences can be detected, although the archipelago's status as a British colony exerts a strong presence, and you will notice an English quality to the infrastructure. Many of the main attractions are in some way connected to the Knights of Malta, as they became known (*see box on p124*).

Constructed to house the Knights of Malta, the **Grand Master's Palace** is elegantly ornate. As well as housing Malta's Parliament, a museum contains a vast range of weapons from the knights' heyday.
Palace Square. Opening times vary. Admission charge.

One of Europe's oldest working theatres, **Manoel Theatre** can be toured, though if you have the

Valletta's Grand Harbour with St John's Co-Cathedral near the shore

opportunity to take in a production in this fabulous venue, it is recommended. Artists to have graced its stage range from Yehudi Menuhin and Mstislav Rostropovich to Clive Owen (on his first appearance for the Young Vic Company) and Steven Berkoff.

115 Old Theatre Street. Tel: (21) 246 389. www.teatrumanoel.com.mt. Tours: Mon–Fri every 45 mins 10.15am–3.30pm, Sat 10.15am–12.30pm. Admission charge.

The influence of the knights and St Paul's shipwreck in Malta have left a legacy of committed Catholicism, and another main group of tourist attractions is churches, of which Malta has over twenty. One of the most important is **St John's Co-Cathedral**, another Knights of Malta creation. Its fort-like exterior captures the duality of the Order – religion and war – while the interior is a stunning sight, with Baroque-style decor fashioned from Maltese limestone. Caravaggio's *The Beheading of Saint John the*

THE KNIGHTS OF MALTA

From humanitarian to military and back again, the Order of St John (or Knights of Malta, or any one of a clutch of other names used), started out as a Christian association. Founded in 1080, it operated a hospital in Jerusalem, tending to needy pilgrims travelling to the Holy Land. Knights came exclusively from wealthy families, greatly enriching the Order. Compassion and charity switched to martial duties in the Crusades, and when the Christians were expelled from the Holy Land the knights moved first to Rhodes, then Malta, of which they were given control. Napoleon's taking of Malta in 1798 dispersed but did not destroy the Order. It later underwent a revival in Britain, and continues to have loosely affiliated branches in Europe.

Baptist is the best of the artwork
on show.
*St John's Square. Tel: (21) 220 536.
www.stjohnscocathedral.com.
Open: Mon–Fri 9.30am–4.30pm,
Sat 9.30am–12.30pm, last admission
half an hour before closing.
Closed: Sun. Admission charge.*

400km (250 miles) southeast of Tunis.

TUNISIA
Tunis
*Ships calling at Tunis dock at La
Goulette, a 40-minute drive from the
capital. The most convenient and best-
value way to get around is to go with a
local minibus operator, who will offer the
same trip as the cruise liner but for a
third or half the price, albeit in a less
luxurious vehicle. You can take a taxi,
but run the risk of being overcharged.*

Tunis has a distinctly Islamic feel

Disembarking in Tunis, you may initially
get surprisingly little sense of being in
Africa. On your way into town you'll
pass a Spanish fortress and a bizarre
mini mock-up of London's Big Ben,
while the architecture is largely French
(an inheritance from France's time as a
colonial power). Nonetheless, the impact
of Islam on people's dress and society at
large (you are unlikely to see a female
trader among the army of male
entrepreneurs), hookah pipes and high
number of smokers plus the odd telling
detail (such as almost every business
displaying a poster of the president) are
unmistakably non-European.

Tunis itself is not overloaded with
must-see sights, but wandering in the
right areas will give you a real sense of
North Africa. A good thoroughfare for
a stroll is the shady Avenue Habib
Bourguiba (named after the country's
post-independence president), with its
pavement cafés. Sit with a mint tea and
watch Tunis go by. The avenue hosts a
couple of prominent buildings, the
**Catholic Cathedral of St Vincent de
Paul**, which dates from the 19th
century (*opening hours vary*), and
opposite it an Art Deco **theatre**.

To up the pace, head for Tunis's main
souk. It has something of the buzz of
Istanbul's Grand Bazaar, but on a
smaller and gentler scale. Here traders
are often too busy manufacturing their
wares on the spot to give potential
customers the hard sell. Arabic music
drifts from the tiny outlets, most of
which are reverentially adorned with

photos of the president. The exotic atmosphere is occasionally punctuated by incongruously modern merchandise such as fake Burberry goods.

Tunis Medina. Open: Sat–Thur 9am–8pm.

Outside the capital, and on the eastern side of Lake Tunis, lies the ancient city of **Carthage**. Razed and re-founded by the Romans, it became one of the top three cities of the Roman Empire, until it was destroyed again in the Muslim Conquest. The ruins, now a UNESCO World Heritage Site, can be visited.

Open: daily 8am–5pm. Admission charge.

On the way to Carthage, you'll pass the atmospheric 2nd-century AD **Colosseum**, where gladiators once did battle. It now hosts plays and concerts.

Open: daily 8am–5pm. Free admission.

400km (250 miles) northwest of Valletta.

ALGERIA
Algiers

Though its tourism industry is nascent compared to that of Tunis or Tangier, Algiers features on some of the more unusual Mediterranean cruise itineraries. The Algerian capital will doubtless increase its profile as travellers' appetites for ever more exotic destinations continue to grow. Its nickname, *Alger la Blanche*, or Algiers the White, makes reference to its whitewashed buildings as viewed from the sea. The city is divided into several districts. The **Casbah** (brought to prominence by the Clash song *Rock the Casbah*) is established on the ruins of old Icosium, and hosts a plethora of historic monasteries in its labyrinthine network of alleyways. Another distinct, **Bab el-Oued**, is popular for its market and workshops.

636km (395 miles) west of Tunis.

Tangier is a very popular destination for day visitors from Spain and Gibraltar

MOROCCO
Tangier

The cruise port is less than 1km (just over half a mile) from the town centre, though there are buses and taxis should you need them.

Exotic and colourful, Tangier occupies the northwest tip of Africa at the Strait of Gibraltar, where the Mediterranean meets the Atlantic. An ethnic cocktail and former resort for the rich (as a tax haven), the city has a cosmopolitan feel while at the same time encapsulating a vivid African vibe.

The hub is the **Medina**, or old city, where an army of artisans go about producing their merchandise, largely leather, shoes and handicrafts. Situated near the harbour, you'll see a grand mosque on the remains of a temple to Neptune, built by the Roman founders. The **Grand Socco** is the lively main square of the medina. Its official name of Place du Avril 1947 commemorates a sultan's visit. The bulk of the retail action is at the **Kasbah**. Be prepared to haggle.

There are places to escape the frenetic hum of the commercial districts. Mosques often enjoy quiet grounds, and calming fountains can often be spotted in serene courtyards. The slightly rundown Hotel Continental, on the edge of the Medina, is the place to go for a panoramic view. Those after cultural pursuits will find several museums and galleries to peruse.

57km (35 miles) southwest of Gibraltar.

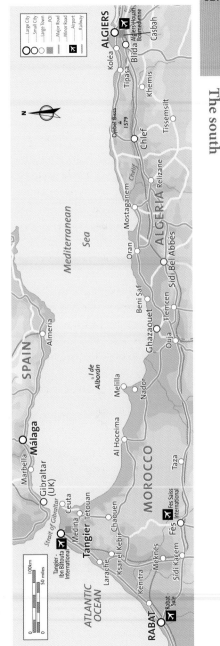

The south

When to go

Balmy Mediterranean weather means that whenever you set sail, you're likely to enjoy plenty of sunshine. While several liners cruise the Med all year long, focusing more on the south during the cold season, others sit out winter, and some split the year between the Mediterranean and the Caribbean or Bahamas, thus maximising operators' revenues. Besides the weather, the other main factor in the timing of your voyage will be financial, as prices can rocket in high season.

An awning on board protects passengers from the heat of the Greek sun

Although the Mediterranean sunshine is often thought of as a given, it's worth paying at least some attention to the climatic aspects of your trip. In high summer, and even during the run-up to it, temperatures can soar on land, particularly in the southern ports, and you may find yourself exploring Athens or Alexandria in over 40°C (104°F). While this may seem wonderful when booking your trip on a miserable February morning back home, it can make hiking up the hill to the Acropolis something of an ordeal. On the other hand, the northern ports are typically cooler, so a look at the various destinations on your itinerary can help you decide when would be the best time to see them.

Land temperatures are just one aspect. You'll also need to consider the time spent on the ship. Despite the mild climate, when the vessel is in motion the wind can inevitably make some of the exposed deck areas feel a bit chilly, particularly those in the shade. So while avoiding high summer might mean that sightseeing is less arduous, you may feel a little cooler as you travel from port to port.

While they can be rather taxing in August, the hotter southern ports come into their own in winter. If you are one of the minority of travellers planning to take to the high seas during the colder months, and would like your trip to be as balmy as possible, it's certainly worth considering Cyprus, the North African coast, Malta and Sicily, where you'll have a much higher chance of sunshine and warmth.

The traditional period for Mediterranean cruising runs from around May to October. Demand and prices peak from around mid-June to the end of August, so if circumstances oblige you to travel at that time, expect to pay extra accordingly. Cruise operators are highly reluctant to sail with a glut of empty cabins, and rather than do so they will slash prices substantially, offering great savings if you can go out of season and book late. The other consideration is how busy the resorts are. Thanks to the price reductions, you're highly unlikely to find yourself on a half-empty boat. But remember that if you're travelling at the height of summer, the more popular ports you visit will be thronging with fellow tourists.

Of course, if you're restricted by work leave or travelling with children on their school holiday, you may have little flexibility. And if you love hot weather, exploring blazing cities may be right up your street. But most other people would certainly benefit from avoiding high season.

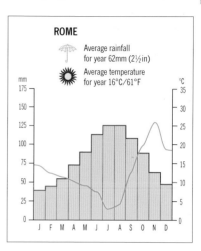

ROME

Average rainfall for year 62mm (2½in)

Average temperature for year 16°C/61°F

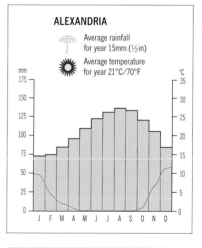

ALEXANDRIA

Average rainfall for year 15mm (½in)

Average temperature for year 21°C/70°F

WEATHER CONVERSION CHART

25.4mm = 1 inch

°F = 1.8 × °C + 32

Getting around

While cruising removes much of the hassle from foreign travel, there remains the issue of how you get around once you leave the boat. Although operators provide their own tours, these are seldom competitively priced, and travellers of an independent bent won't enjoy traipsing around to a set itinerary with several dozen other tourists in tow. It's possible to go it alone, but how easy that is varies from country to country and port to port.

Official tours

Once on-board, you are a captive audience, and cruise operators vigorously promote their own excursions. You're likely to be given a talk on what outings are available (often craftily merged with the obligatory safety briefing so there is no escape!). The official line will sometimes contain a few horror stories of fellow tourists having been mercilessly ripped off by rogue taxi drivers, who, knowing the ship's departure time, practically held their naïve passengers to ransom. What the ship staff will probably not tell you is that there is almost always a cheaper way to do the exact same tour independently if you prefer.

Of course, taking the official tour is not without advantages. In certain ports, particularly (but by no means limited to) the North African ones, a foreign tourist does run a risk of being overcharged by unscrupulous local merchants. While it's usually possible to

avoid that eventuality with a few simple precautions (such as researching in advance the local currency exchange rate and roughly what things should cost, and negotiating any taxi fare in advance), it can be a worry, and many travellers simply prefer to avoid the aggravation by booking the official excursion. The other classic fear is missing the boat. On the cruise's own day trip, you have peace of mind that, if there is an unavoidable delay, the ship has to wait for you. Explore independently and it might not. If you have mobility issues, you may also prefer to travel with the cruise liner's tour, where certain standards are guaranteed. However, in general, these tours are overpriced and it's perfectly possible to have an equivalent (or better) experience for less money.

Local tours

In some ports, a good alterative is a locally organised tour. These are often quite well run and sometimes work on

A group of tourists approaches the quay at Maó harbour, Menorca

an unofficial basis with the ship staff. Local operators will be waiting when the ship arrives, and approach disembarking passengers with their offer. If the individual or company is known to the liner's disembarkation staff members, they may even direct independently travelling passengers towards the operator's bus. This is reassuring, as the operator knows that if their service falls below par, passengers will report this back to the ship, and the casual cooperation would be over. Such a set-up is more likely in a small port that sees fewer cruise ships.

In larger ports it's still sometimes possible to find alternative excursions, although the providers are unlikely to coordinate as closely with your cruise as they would in a smaller stopover. Minibus drivers greet passengers, and state their price for taking them to the local attractions. Always check whether the fare includes the return journey, or whether you would need to find your own way back to the port.

One advantage of these unofficial excursions is financial – you may pay as little as a third or a half what the ship's own day trip would cost you. They can be more intimate, too. There are likely to be fewer passengers with you, so your group will not swamp the attractions it visits. And the tour is often quirkier and less polished, which can appeal to the kind of traveller who enjoys experiencing the more unusual, less sanitised aspects of a destination.

Of course, you do assume a slight risk by eschewing the ship-endorsed expedition for one of this kind. While the ship would probably wait if a group of its passengers was unavoidably delayed, it would not be obliged to do so for one or two people. But more adventurous passengers often feel the advantages outweigh such a small risk.

Taxi

Another way to get around is by local taxi, and most ports have a line of drivers waiting outside to snap up exiting passengers. Travel by taxi and you have maximum flexibility – go exactly where you want, stay as long as you feel like and do so without the

Taxis are not usually hard to find – here in Lisbon

tourist hordes in close attendance. A cab can be a cheaper option than the ship excursion, or much more expensive – it is contingent on a variety of factors including the distances involved, the costs of the country you're in, your haggling skills, how rich you look and so forth.

If the fare is negotiated in advance or a meter used, a taxi can be a convenient way to make the most out of the short time you have at your destination. But there are risks. Fail to establish the fare before setting off in a taxi without a meter, and at the end of your journey you may be met with an astronomical charge and/or an unseemly argument. If you're rushing to get back for departure and a cowboy cab driver knows it, you might find yourself in a bad spot. While such encounters may be more common in North Africa, it would be equally possible to find yourself being ripped off in a supposedly safer European Union country. So do consider the risks and issues before hopping in a cab.

Hire car

If you don't want to rely on an unknown driver, you could consider hiring a car. Many ports have outlets in or around the terminal. Things to consider are the driving conditions and regulations in each country.

Public transport

Adventurous types or those on a tight budget may prefer to get around by public transport. In Europe, especially, there is often a well-integrated system. Not only can you see places at a fraction of the cost of a tour, but you'll also be travelling with local people, which can be a refreshing change from the sanitised atmosphere of the cruise, where the majority of people may be of your own nationality. On the downside, the extra time taken can limit what you can see, and you need to plan your journey carefully – a delayed or cancelled service could leave you stranded.

Walking

If you don't wish to stray far, and the ship is docked near town, there may be no need for any transport at all.

Open-top buses tour many of the cities and are a good way to see round a place in a short time

Food and drink

The health-giving powers of the Mediterranean diet have been much trumpeted in recent years, and they are frequently cited as the secret behind the pockets of longevity throughout the region. That said, the region is home to a culinary patchwork, from the spices of the North African coast to European standards such as pasta and tapas. Ship fare, too, can be a highlight of your trip.

On board

Operators know that their audience is captive (there's no popping out for a takeaway), and most strive to make sure that dining is a positive part of your holiday. Despite its romantic and nostalgic appeal, dinner with the captain does not typically feature on most cruises (given that there may be several thousand passengers aboard, he would have to spend a lot of time eating!). But some ships still offer formal dining, and even the more casual have spruced up their menus, sometimes with the help of celebrity chefs.

Menus can vary wildly, from the trendy (think edamame beans), to the traditional (steak and chips). Ship caterers usually ensure that there are plenty of options from the national cuisine of the majority of passengers. Buffets are often used to accommodate the large numbers of passengers all requiring feeding at once. At the higher end of the market, formal dining (yes, sometimes at the captain's table) is

more prevalent. Here meals may be served in sittings, and à la carte. Where space allows, lower-cost cruises may also have a special, à la carte restaurant, with a separate charge (buffet dining would normally be included in the overall cruise price). These are increasingly adventurous in their theme, serving up sushi and similar dishes, and it's often advisable to book ahead. Despite the limitations of galley (the ship's kitchen) cookery, high standards are often achieved. At the other end of the scale, the most basic ships may offer a limited buffet, or the choice of a handful of pre-prepared dishes. Vegetarians are usually well catered for, though on cheaper cruises their choices may be limited.

Times of eating again depend on the ship. Some may offer 24-hour dining, others specific meal times. In the latter case, breakfast is generally served from around 7am to 9am or 10am, lunch from approximately noon to 2.30pm and dinner anywhere between 6pm and

10pm. It's usually possible to have your own table, although there are generally larger tables too, for big groups and anyone who feels like being sociable. Hygiene is taken very seriously, and you may be (politely) squirted with antiseptic handwash on your way into the restaurant or dining hall. A bout of food poisoning is perhaps one of the worst adverts for a cruise liner. Tipping etiquette varies widely from ship to ship; if you're concerned, check online

Enjoy local mussels and fine wines on the Côte d'Azur

Food and drink

or in one of the detailed cruising manuals. Most ship restaurants are non-smoking, with an area for smokers provided close by.

On shore

While cruise ship food is often great, the true delights of cruising the Med lie in experiencing its varied cuisines. Given that everywhere you eat when ashore will be at or near a port, of particular quality will be the fresh fish. Fish is a staple of the 'Mediterranean diet', which has been praised for reducing rates of numerous illnesses including cancer, heart disease, Alzheimer's, diabetes and asthma. The diet is also characterised by high consumption of olive oil, fruit and veg, nuts and grains, and a little red wine.

Of course, there are regional variations. Though it doesn't border the Med, Portuguese cuisine is considered a good example of the diet. Its rich and flavoursome dishes betray Arab and Moorish traits, particularly in the prevalence of spice. Olive oil, garlic and herbs are common. Spain is famous chiefly for paella (a rice dish) and tapas (mixed appetisers), and seafood is very popular. Sangria, a sweetened fruit punch, is served in both Portugal and Spain.

A giant on the world culinary scene is France. Exquisitely prepared mussels are likely to be a highlight of your Côte d'Azur dining, perhaps washed down with a glass of champagne or one of the country's other highly esteemed wines. Like that of its neighbour, Italian

Tempting seafood and wine on display at a restaurant in Syros

Local wine for sale in Cannes

cuisine needs little introduction – its pizza and pasta are known and consumed pretty much the world over; likewise its coffee. However, many are unaware of the significant regional variations. Sicilian and Sardinian gastronomies are dominated by fish, the former also influenced by ingredients introduced by Arab traders.

Croatian cuisine, far less familiar, varies by region, with its coastal fare a simple take on Italian and French gastronomy, and rich in fish. Moving south and east, Greek food is often held up as a standard-bearer for the Mediterranean diet, with olive oil practically ubiquitous. Vegetables, including tomato and aubergine, feature prominently, and dishes are often enlivened with herbs. Cheeses in Greece are many and varied, including feta, which crops up in the signature Greek salad. There is also plenty of fish to be had. Crete's cuisine is often considered an embodiment of the Mediterranean diet, and its isolated communities have frequently been used for research by nutritionists and scientists, eager to learn the secrets of Cretans' resilience to certain ailments. Turkey unites Mediterranean fare with Middle Eastern influences, with the most famous dish probably the kebab. As elsewhere, the olive oil flows freely.

In North Africa, things become spicier, thanks in the main to the cinnamon, saffron, nutmeg, ginger and cloves introduced by Arab traders. Many dishes can be found again and again along the coast, sometimes with almost the same name. Berber and European influences are also distinguishable. Vegetable-heavy and easy on the meat, Egyptian food will suit vegetarians and even vegans. Seafood also features heavily in the coastal areas. As along the North African coast, Malta's cuisine is a mélange of the many nationalities who found their way to the island.

Food shopping

The countries with more developed tourism have cottoned on to the global mania for the Mediterranean diet. Here you'll find shops with tempting and beautifully packaged arrays of olive oil, wine, sweets, plus other local delicacies. They make excellent, and great-value, gifts – if you can bear to part with them once home!

Entertainment

When passages at sea can last for over 24 hours at a stretch, cruise companies must go to lengths to ensure their passengers don't get bored. On a large ship, you might find various amusements competing for your time, and even smaller vessels try to put on some form of entertainment. On shore, of course, there are myriad cafés, bars, restaurants, theatres, music venues and cinemas awaiting exploration.

On board

Casinos and games of chance

The siting of casinos on boats was a handy way to circumvent restrictive gaming legislation in the United States, and the association has endured, with plenty of cruise ships featuring them. Gamblers will usually find a decent range of slot machines and tables, and things are run as professionally as they would be at a land-based casino. Ships that regularly see a large contingent of older, British passengers also offer bingo.

Dancing

Most ships have some kind of place where their passengers can strut their stuff – either a small dance floor in one of the public rooms or a dedicated disco replete with glitter ball. The music will be geared towards the majority demographic of the clientele: typically the latest dance tunes for teenagers and twenty-somethings, retro for those hovering around middle age and more serene melodies for the older cohort. Cruises that get a large number of older, single, female passengers often employ personable male hosts to partner them on the dance floor.

Language lessons

The week or two you're on board is not going to be long enough to turn you into a polyglot, but if there's a bilingual member of staff on board, a language lesson may be offered to allow you to learn just enough holiday vocabulary to impress the locals when you dock.

Quizzes

Perhaps owing to the ease of arranging it and its cross-generational appeal, the quiz is a popular pastime on cruise ships. From large and highly organised affairs with visual aids and prizes, to small, just-for-fun varieties, a cruise usually gives you a chance to test your knowledge of trivia.

Entertainers on board an Ocean Village cruise ship

Quoits

It might belong to the nostalgic selection of cruise images that includes dinner with the captain and Agatha Christie mysteries, but quoits is still alive and well on ship decks throughout the Mediterranean. Participants stand at a distance and try to throw a ring to land over a pin.

Restaurants, cafés and bars

Depending on the size of the ship, there may be several on-board cafés, restaurants, bars and clubs in which to pass the time. Some crafts have café concessions, allowing you to pick up your favourite high-street coffee on the high seas. The atmosphere of such places is contingent on the ship size and clientele. A large liner will have a range of places catering to all tastes: a lively bar for the party crowd, with the odd karaoke night, a piano café, often with some live jazz or mellow pop, for the more laidback holidaymaker, a quiet spot where you can enjoy a cuppa, and so on. A smaller vessel will offer less choice, but there will always be somewhere to enjoy a drink or snack.

Shows

Lack of space will probably preclude this on a smaller ship, but larger vessels stage a variety of shows. While the cruise-ship circuit has been maligned as the career graveyard for performers, it is actually possible to see some top-class shows while you sail. All manner of entertainment is staged. Trapeze artists and other circus performers cavort around the ship. Various musicians will step up to the mike. Some resident performers often do three gigs a day in a large liner's various venues, while other acts (often tribute) stay a night or two performing before departing for another ship. Magicians and comedians also take to the stage, and usually do a gig or two before leaving. If the material veers towards the risqué, the show will be staged late at night and a warning given. Some operators go all out and stage deck-side extravaganzas with sound, light and snazzily-costumed performers performing breathtaking stunts reminiscent of a Las Vegas spectacle. You will also occasionally find a cinema on board.

A jazz singer entertains in the lobby of a cruise ship

On shore

The extraordinary cultural heritage of the Mediterranean ensures a plethora of ways to entertain yourself during your time on shore.

Folk music and dance

While organised evening entertainment might not fit with your ship's schedule, it is often easier to catch some local folk music or dance. The smaller ports sometimes lay on a small-scale display for disembarking or re-embarking passengers, with a handful of dancers or musicians providing a flavour of the local rhythms. In the larger, more vibrant cities, you could be lucky enough to spot street exhibitions – flamenco dancers in Barcelona, say. It may also be possible to combine folk with food, from Portugal's dedicated *fado* restaurants to the house bands employed by some Greek restaurateurs.

Restaurants, cafés and bars

One of the first ports of call following disembarkation, as well as after a hot day's sightseeing, will be a stop for refreshments. Sitting in a local café or restaurant, watching the sea lap the shore or the world go by, can be a great pleasure. The kinds of café are as varied as the destinations: sip a mint tea in a souk in Tunis, knock back an authentic espresso in an Italian café in Naples, sip on sangria in Barcelona, close your eyes and enjoy an ouzo on a Greek island… While the liner is docked you'll almost certainly take one meal a day on shore,

One of the street entertainments in La Rambla, Barcelona

so there is plenty of time to sample the local eateries.

Theatre, opera, cinema, concerts

How far this is applicable depends greatly on the kind of cruise you have opted for. If your ship ever stays docked overnight, you'll have the time to enquire about what's on and perhaps take in a show, whether it's an open-air film on a Greek island or a performance at Rome's Teatro dell'Opera. If this is an important part of your trip, it's a good idea to research this ahead of time, as the more popular shows can obviously sell out in advance. If, however, your cruise is more geared towards daytime exploration and always sets sail before dusk, this might be more difficult.

Shopping

While a ship might not have a huge amount of space to devote to retail, cruise operators often try to optimise this source of revenue with on-board shops, and a non-EU shop allows for duty-free goods. But your best holiday shopping is likely to be done on shore. Journeying from country to country and port to port lets you browse a wide selection of souvenirs, often representing great value.

On board

On-board retail outlets range from small shops selling sun cream, beach paraphernalia, toiletries and ship souvenirs to something resembling a shopping mall. Despite the fact that duty-free goods are available if the ship docks outside the EU, prices can be high. Events such as art auctions attempt to make a feature of certain goods. Duty-free shops must remain closed while in port by law.

On shore

The Mediterranean region encompasses a range of retail experiences, from quirky markets to polished, tourist-oriented boutiques. Local entrepreneurs have cannily realised what kind of souvenir the foreign traveller wants and tend to flag up what is best or distinctive about the destination: olive oil and its offshoot products, confectionery, wine, delicacies like Greek honey, spices, upmarket toiletries, ornaments, calendars, books and so on.

A less refined but more colourful shopping experience is the local market, or souk, as it is called in North Africa. Selling leather goods, fabrics, clothes, crockery, gold, jewellery and woodcraft, this is a retail outlet where tough haggling is required. But, even if you don't want to buy anything, the bustling Arab atmosphere is enjoyable in itself; sit in one of the small cafés with a tea and watch the traders at work.

What to buy

The Mediterranean region offers the souvenir shopper a huge amount of choice. Popular buys include consumables. Olive oil is a good memento of your trip – particularly as the Mediterranean Basin is sometimes defined as where the olive tree grows. The high-quality wines of France and Italy are another treat representative of the region. Jars of honey or olives are delicious as well as portable. The eastern and southern nations' heavy use

Lanterns on sale in Tunis

of flavouring in their cuisine has also made packaged spices a common and colourful purchase.

The legacy of trade between states in the area means that away from the world of food and drink there are plenty of other products to buy. Clothes can be picked up everywhere, from the designer shops of the South of France and Italy (best visited in July and August during the sales) to the bargains of Turkey and chichi tourist boutiques on the Greek islands. Rugs and carpets are characteristic of much of North Africa, Turkey, Greece and Spain, and various fabrics also dot the shops and markets of Croatia and Portugal. If you're after leather, the best bets are Turkey, Greece, Italy, Morocco and other parts of North Africa, Spain and Portugal. For jewellery, try Egypt, Morocco, Croatia and Turkey. Handicrafts and ceramics can be sourced from most of the less developed places, including the North African coast, Turkey and Greece. And for something that will be entirely useless once you get it home, but will provide an excellent talking point, go for the weird and wonderful: a belly dancing costume from Egypt or a hookah pipe from Turkey.

Sport and leisure

A gym might not be the first thing a novice cruiser would associate with a ship, but they are now, along with pools, fairly de rigueur. Other facilities will depend on the size of the liner. As in tourism generally, spas have mushroomed throughout the industry, and rare is the boat where you can't get a mid-sea massage. Cycling, meanwhile, is a convenient way of exploring ports and their surrounds.

On board

Most passengers will want to take to – or at least sit by – the pool during their voyage. Space limitations preclude Olympic-size pools; most will be on the small side, but will suffice for a quick dip in what is generally filtered salt water. If there is room, you may find separate pools for children and adults, and family-oriented cruise operators might also install slides and wave machines. There is usually a whirlpool or two in the vicinity of the pool.

The other leisure fixture on board is the gym, which will come equipped with treadmills, bikes, weights and so on – in short, everything you'd expect in a typical land-based facility. Use of the equipment is generally free, even on lower-cost cruises. A space will probably be set aside for activities such as Pilates or yoga, though a separate charge is often made for classes. Ship gyms usually get allotted a decent location on the boat, so your workout will be to a background of sea views.

The same is true of spas, which can sometimes be found bang in the middle of the front of the boat. Two companies dominate the cruise-ship spa scene, Steiner Leisure and the On-boardSpa Company. Again, given the limitations, ship spas are usually well equipped with various treatment, meditation and relaxation rooms – and a full menu of beauty and health treatments from which to choose.

Other recreational facilities run the spectrum from humble to huge. At the more basic end of the scale, ships sometimes have table tennis, quoits, shuffleboard, basketball and volleyball courts, plus a few video games for children. The big players boast everything from running tracks and rock-climbing walls to surfing and golf simulators, rollerblading and ice-skating rinks.

On shore

Keen cyclists often have the option of 'doing' the port by bike. The official

Playing volleyball on a Kos beach

cruise excursion menu sometimes includes an organised cycling tour, which allows you to cover a large amount of the destination without recourse to the ship-organised tour bus, taxis or public transport. Routes are usually graded by difficulty.

Beach destinations afford the opportunity to snorkel, and possibly scuba-dive. You're likely to find local operators catering to this demand around the beach or possibly near the port. Boat journeys to local islands – if your appetite for the open wave has not been sated – can also sometimes be undertaken, and offer a pleasant way to put some distance between you and your cruise mates, should you wish. Other activities depend on the destination.

Children

Received wisdom might have it that children don't mix well with the traditional cruising cohort, but there are many reasons why a Mediterranean cruise can make an ideal family holiday. The enclosed environment presents obvious security advantages, with everyone on board being known and identifiable, whether passenger or staff member. In their race for revenue, cruise companies are always expanding their range of facilities, and today's young seafarers will be besieged with entertainment options.

The golden rule is to pick your ship carefully. The least child-friendly ships de-select themselves: several are adults only. But the vessels that allow children on board do varying amounts to keep them amused. In general, the larger ships have more facilities. Children may have dedicated computer games rooms, discos, theatres, swimming pools and playgrounds. Kids' clubs are operational on many craft, and some will take care of your little darlings all day, allowing you to discover the port at your leisure. You can sometimes avail yourself of on-board babysitting services too. If you're looking forward to the break, it's important to check details in advance – some services have age limits or require a parent to be present with toddlers. Check the cost too: some services are free; others are not.

It's unlikely that you'll want to deposit your brood in the kids' club for the entirety of your cruise: the Mediterranean affords a wonderful variety of ports and excursions to amuse and entertain children. Pyramids, the Leaning Tower of Pisa, Venice's network of canals, brightly coloured North African markets – this type of varied fun should stifle the dreaded whine of 'I'm bored'. Plus there is always the fallback of splashing around on the beach and irrigating a sandcastle with the incoming tide.

In terms of practical problems, cruises are generally reassuring. The absence of any strangers on board (the comings and goings of crew and passengers are monitored via swipe card) allows parents to relax, and there are sometimes sectioned-off parent and child areas for further peace of mind (and probably to avoid annoying adult passengers!). A doctor will be on hand for health problems. The ship's shop should stock the bare necessities. Exemplary hygiene standards allow you to enjoy your meal without fear of upset stomachs – often a worry on multi-stop foreign trips – and the cruise restaurant menu will usually include the bland

Children

Children will love the beaches around the Mediterranean, here at Cannes

options and perennial favourites beloved of kids. It is sometimes possible to purchase a pass at the start of your trip that gives your child a special cup entitling them to free drinks for the remainder of the holiday.

Cost will be a consideration for many, and the prohibitive pricing of cruising in the past probably contributed to the absence of young passengers. But the excellent rates on budget cruises have changed all that. Today, a week's family holiday sailing the Mediterranean can be surprisingly economical (provided you go easy on the official ship excursions, that is). Add to that the chance to spend some time away from your offspring without too high a level of anxiety, and a slew of educational attractions and the appeal is clear.

Cruising and cruise ships

Cruise liners are often thought of as floating hotels, and indeed some do afford their guests a similar degree of luxury and level of service. But a ship is a machine, and as such some aspects of your holiday will differ markedly from the average jaunt through Europe. The following outlines what the novice cruiser should expect and gives some pointers on the types of vessels that cruise the Mediterranean.

Ships come in one shape but various sizes, from modest vessels transporting barely over a hundred passengers to nautical behemoths carrying upwards of 3,000 holiday-makers. But all share a few essentials. The ship's command centre is the bridge, a raised platform from where the course is plotted and vessel steered. This is where the captain is to be found, but he (it's still a male-dominated profession) often delegates the donkey work of steering at sea to somebody else. Bridges are serene and often delightfully old-fashioned, with the crew relying on paper charts and computers that look as if they were manufactured in the 1980s rather than flashy state-of-the-art navigational technology. Few passengers have the chance to visit the bridge (owing to security risks as well as the impracticability of ushering hundreds of people through in the course of a week or so). But there are occasional tours, and you might be lucky. The engine room – or machinery space as it is sometimes termed – is usually situated towards the back of the ship, and is off

limits for obvious reasons. Next to it may be the engine control room.

The swimming pool(s) is/are on the top deck, sometimes overlooked by an upper viewing level. This area is also usually home to the gym and spa, creating a recreational space. Depending on how many restaurants the vessel contains, one of the speciality ones, or even the main one, might be

CRUISE ARGOT

Cruise ships are an environment removed from the everyday and, like many such, they have their own vernacular. Forget left and right, it's port and starboard (although sadly the story that the word 'posh' derives from the ship shorthand Port Out Starboard Home is apocryphal). The front and back have even more synonyms: fore, forward or bow and aft or stern respectively. 'Bilge' refers to the interior of the hull below the floor, rather than nonsense. Ships have galleys, not kitchens. They also have 'heads' not toilets (not to be confused with the poop deck, which is something else entirely!). But the number one rule on the ship must be: don't call it a boat! Seasoned cruisers and crew consider the term disrespectful for such a substantial vessel.

up here too. A kitchen area – which, given the huge demand, must work at optimum efficiency – will adjoin it.

Cabins line the sides of the craft. Clearly economic viability relies on packing as many passengers in as possible, so on all but the grandest liners there are two rows of cabins along each side of the ship, one of which doesn't have a window. These quarters are termed 'inside cabins', and are the cheapest place to stay on the ship. Cruise companies do all sorts of things to distract from the weirdness of a windowless room, such as hanging curtains or putting artwork there.

Enjoying an early evening drink and a wonderful view from the deck, here near Palma de Mallorca

'Outside cabins' stand opposite the inside cabins. These are identical to their inside counterparts, except for the presence of either a picture window or a porthole. Cabins are invariably small and may come with double, twin or bunk beds, the latter particularly if the room accommodates more than two passengers.

Moving up the ship accommodation hierarchy, we come to the self-explanatory 'balcony cabins'. Bear in mind that your balcony may be visible from others in the vicinity. Aside from the outside space, which is sometimes fashioned from the accommodation space itself, the cabin will differ little from its cheaper peers. Top of the heap is the suite. The word does not necessarily apply in the hotel sense: there might not be separate sleeping quarters. However, suites are spacious, and the very swankiest come with dining areas, sizeable outside decks and even whirlpools. Price gradation reflects these four categories, as well as other factors such as how high up the cabin is (you pay for the better view – although be prepared to experience rough seas more intensively than your shipmates lower down). The same is true if you're right at the front of the ship, where you might also have to endure anchor noise; cabins at the back might experience engine noise.

The level of the entrance and exit will vary depending on the port; staff will usually put up signs directing you to the correct deck, and you'll probably

A standard double cabin

hear announcements over the speaker system too. Embarkation and disembarkation may be done by ramp or – depending on the port layout, traffic and weather – by tender, meaning small shuttle boats. Boarding them can be tricky, but the crew will help. Though you wouldn't think it when you're out on the open waves, ships can suffer the same traffic jams as other forms of transport, and if the port is busy you may have to wait your turn before your ship can dock and disembarkation can begin.

Another aspect that will reinforce the difference between a cruise and standard holiday is the safety briefing. Your presence is mandatory – if you don't turn up your name will be noted and you will be summoned over the speaker system to attend a repeat. While the ostensible purpose of this is so you are fully conversant in safety and evacuation procedures, you may also get the excursion sales pitch.

The resemblance of cruise ships to hotels raises another issue for many: tipping. Passengers often want clarification on how much should be given, and to whom, but unfortunately there are no comprehensive answers. While staff on some ships will expect tips, other cruise liners – mindful, perhaps, of the potential awkwardness the whole business can engender – include tips in the total fare, and no further dispensing of gratuities is expected. Contrastingly, some liners will put envelopes under your door while others add a surcharge to your various purchases as you go.

Cruise lines price guide

★   Budget

★★   Moderate

★★★   Moderately expensive

★★★★ Top end

Prices are for two people on the cheapest tariff available (so usually for an inside cabin), in mid- to high season. However, the categories indicated should be taken only as a very rough guide. Prices fluctuate dramatically depending on season and, more importantly, demand, as no liner wants to sail with empty cabins. Canny booking could therefore secure you, say, a cabin on a three-star ship for a category one-star fare. Alternatively, unusually high demand could do the opposite.

easyCruise ★

Taking the no-frills concept onto the high seas, easyCruise's two small ships operate short-duration voyages that focus on the Greek islands. The budget and the party ethos (the ship often stays docked late into the night and arrivals tend to be late morning) suit a younger crowd. But the excellent value for money wins fans from across all demographics, and Brits and Americans mingle with natives of Greece (the home port is Athens). Flights are not included.
Tel: 0871 210 0001.
www.easycruise.com

Costa Cruises ★★

With a large and rapidly growing fleet, Costa plies destinations all around the Med. Facilities are modern and the style is Italian, reflecting the company's heritage (it transported fabrics and olive oil in the 19th century).
Tel: 020 7940 5398.
www.costacruises.co.uk

A reception desk on board an Ocean Village cruise ship

Cruising and cruise ships

Passengers enjoy the pool deck while their ship sails by Paros

Norwegian Cruise Line ★★

Appropriately for a Nordic-named company, Norwegian Cruise Line places the emphasis on fitness facilities. Entertainment is also a big deal. Large suites and interconnecting rooms appeal to family groups, and the flexible dining suits more independent types. Circular cruises emanate mainly from Barcelona, and there are eastern Mediterranean cruises in winter. Day stops are the norm, but there's the odd overnighter on longer sojourns.
Tel (US): (001) 866 234 7350.
www.ncl.com

Ocean Village ★★

Priding itself on its laidback and flexible ethos, Ocean Village's slogan is 'the cruise for people who don't do cruises'. Two large ships spend the summer months plying the eastern and western Mediterranean regions. Week- and fortnight-long trips cater to a mainly British clientele. The vessel arrives early in the morning and usually leaves by 6pm. Flights to the European departure port are normally included.
Tel: 0845 075 0032.
www.oceanvillageholidays.co.uk

Carnival Cruises ★★★

Fun and informal cruising (think Las Vegas at sea). Carnival's casual style attracts active, participatory sorts. Med cruises depart mainly from Rome, and follow a circular route. Ships arrive on the early side and berth for the day.

Tel (US): (001) 800 227 6482.
www.carnival.com

P&O Cruises ★★★

Pioneer P&O has been in the pleasure cruise market since 1837 and is one of the big names in the business. Slightly traditional in feel (think afternoon tea, no Wi-Fi and shorts frowned upon at dinner), some of its fleet cater to adults only. Cruises of various durations start from Southampton. Daytime stops are the norm.
Tel: 0845 678 0014. www.pocruises.com

Princess Cruises ★★★

Princess stands out for its excellent range of facilities for passengers with disabilities. Its large vessels do a variety of Mediterranean routes, both circular and one-way. Middle-aged Americans are the main cohort on board, and there is a degree of formality expected. The ships also cater for children.
Tel (US): (001) 661 753 0000.
www.princess.com

Passengers taking a good look at Livorno port

Windstar Cruises ★★★

Windstar's quirky looking vessels (cruise ships with sails on the top) shuttle back and forth between Athens and Greece. Their diminutive size ensures an intimate atmosphere and also allows for stops in ports that are too small for large liners. The intimacy suits couples looking for romance, and those who want an upmarket environment but to dress down. Watersports feature prominently, but there's less in the way of noisy activities. *Tel (US): (001) 800 258 7245.* *www.windstarcruises.com*

There is plenty of seating provided on deck

Royal Caribbean ★★★/★★★★

Several of this line's colossal vessels do one-way and circular Med cruises, berthing during the day. Royal Caribbean is known in the business for its improbable features, such as rock-climbing walls, ice rinks and bungee trampolines. It's also one of the few cruise lines that allows you to play pool, thanks to self-levelling table technology. *Tel (US): (001) 866 562 7625.* *www.royalcaribbean.com*

Celebrity Cruises ★★★★

Every bit as glitzy as the name suggests, Celebrity offers fine dining, chic add-ons like a martini bar and a butler service for the highest-paying passengers. The atmosphere is fairly quiet, and there is plenty of modern art to admire if that's your cup of tea. Fortunately, prices are not quite as high as the upscale decor and service might suggest. There are several circular itineraries for the region. *Tel (US): (001) 800 647 2251.* *www.celebritycruises.com*

Cunard Line ★★★★

Cunard is the *grande dame* of Mediterranean – indeed all – cruising and has been since 1838. Ships depart from Southampton (or New York) with daytime port stops. Regally titled vessels – whose names are so well known that the initials, QE2, QM2, will suffice – come with all manner of posh trappings. The atmosphere is, unsurprisingly, formal and the clientele well-heeled. *Tel: 0845 071 0300. www.cunard.com*

A Costa Cruise ship approaches Mykonos harbour

Essentials

Arriving and departing

When booking, most companies will offer you the choice of having flights included or 'cruise only', where you have to make your own way to the port. The benefit of the former is the convenience of departing from your home country and being transferred straight to the port.

If you drive to the port, make enquiries in advance about parking. It's often possible to book secure parking close to the terminal at a discount. Ship staff may know little about parking options, and terminal staff exhibit varying levels of comprehension and helpfulness.

Checking in is a relatively painless procedure, although there can be queues. Security is taken seriously – it is more akin to an airport than a floating hotel. You will be photographed, so nobody can board the ship using your swipe card. Because most ships operate on a strict weekly timetable, the arrival/departure day may feel a little rushed. If you board early you might not have immediate access to your cabin, as cleaning might still be in progress. A week later, you might find yourself being ushered out of your room earlier than you wish.

Customs

Customs formalities are usually conducted in the port terminal. Precise laws and limits vary from country to country, so check in advance. Your cruise line can often provide some broad information.

Electricity

Ships normally have a mixture of continental European two-pin and British three-pin plug sockets. If the majority of passengers are from the UK, this kind will usually predominate.

Internet

Most (but not all) cruise ships now offer internet access, either through on-board terminals or Wi-Fi. However, it is usually extortionately priced (though you can reduce the cost a little by buying a packet of one or two hours), and the use of satellites can affect its reliability. Unless it's an emergency, it's usually better to wait until you dock. Some port terminals have internet access.

Language

Portuguese, Spanish, Catalan, French, Italian, Croatian, Greek, Turkish, Egyptian, Arabic and Maltese are the main official languages spoken in the countries covered in this book; a handful of minority tongues are also recognised. But English is widely understood and spoken in Mediterranean destinations, particularly in the towns more used to accommodating tourists, so you probably won't need a library of phrasebooks.

Money

Most ships operate on a cash-free basis, where you charge all purchases to your swipe card and pay off the balance at the end of your holiday. Of course, the Mediterranean mainland does not operate on a cash-free basis! A large bloc of countries that feature on cruise itineraries, including Portugal, Spain, France, Italy, Greece, Cyprus and Malta, have adopted the Euro. The other main currencies in use in the destinations covered by this book are the Gibraltar pound, Croatian kuna, Turkish lira, Egyptian pound, Tunisian dinar, Algerian dinar and Moroccan dirham. In practice, many businesses outside the Euro zone are also happy to accept Euros, although the Euro is not their official currency. You can generally change money at your ship reception. On shore, ATM accessibility and the presence of *bureaux de change* vary from place to place, but ports are normally geared up to the arrival of foreign visitors.

Opening hours

While on-board restaurants, bars, spas, gyms, casinos and so forth tend to keep fairly predictable hours, the one exception may be shops. Required by law to remain closed while the ship is docked, retail outlets sometimes make up for this by staying open late into the night. Larger ships are more likely to have 24-hour facilities.

Off the boat, opening hours vary, with the most obvious difference that while in Christian countries businesses are more likely to be closed on Sunday, the Muslim holy day is Friday.

In Spain and Portugal, banks start the day at 8.30am and finish around 2 or 3pm on weekdays, with Spanish banks also opening on Saturday morning during the winter. Shops open at 9 or 9.30am, and stay open until 7 or 8pm from Monday to Friday; Saturday opening hours sometimes run to early afternoon. Bear in mind that things may shut down for Spanish siesta between 2 and 5pm; the Portuguese are also partial to a long lunch. Museums tend to remain shut on Monday. Gibraltar generally sticks to British hours, with shops open from approximately 9am to 6pm, and early closing on Saturday.

France's variable banking hours range from opening times of 9 or 10am to closing at 4 to 5.30pm on weekdays, sometimes with a lunch break. Banks may open Saturday morning and are sometimes shut on Monday. Shops, also individualistic in their schedules, tend to operate from Monday to Saturday from around 9am to 6 or 7pm, sometimes with a lunch break. Similarly inconsistent, Italian opening hours roughly mirror France's. Banks operate from 8 or 8.30 to 4 or 4.30pm on weekdays with a lunch break, plus some Saturday mornings. Shops trade from around 8.30am to 7.30pm, sometimes with a siesta. In both countries, museums tend to close on Monday (and sometimes Tuesday in France).

Croatians make an early start with banks and shops open on weekdays from 7.30 or 8am through to 7pm, and morning trading on Saturday. Cypriots are also early risers, though precise opening times vary greatly by the season and day of the week. Often erratic Greek business hours see banks open around 8.30 and close at 2pm from Monday to Thursday, slightly earlier on Friday. Shops are open from 9am to 9pm or later six days a week, with a long siesta in summer. Turks work from 8 or 9am to 5pm, later in Istanbul.

Banks and shops in Egypt keep long hours, from 8.30 or 9am to 8, 9 or 10pm, with a siesta. Friday tends to be the closed day. Tunisian banks are open every day except Sunday, from 8am or so to 6 or 7pm, with a long lunch. Shops stay open later with a shorter break, with souks often trading daily. Algerian businesses operate from 7.30 or 8.30am to 5.30pm, staying shut on Friday. Moroccan banks are open from about 8.30am to 4.30 pm with a long lunch; some businesses are closed on Friday. Facilities in Muslim countries may be affected by Ramadan. In more cruise-oriented destinations, local hours are adapted to cater to passengers.

Passports and visas

Visa requirements depend on your itinerary. EU citizens can move freely between member states, while Americans, Canadians, Australians and New Zealanders can spend 90 days in the bloc, without a visa. South Africans, however, do require a visa. If your cruise stops outside the EU, you'll need to check the visa rules. It can be a case of simply buying one at the port terminal, but in some places there may be some bureaucracy. Sometimes the cruise line can organise group visas.

Some cruise companies take your passport at check-in and keep it for the entirety of your trip. Others give it back to you once the formalities are complete.

Pharmacies

A ship's medical centre may have some basic provisions – there may even be an on-board pharmacy – but still take with you any medication you normally use.

Post

Stamps can be bought on most ships, and staff will post your mail at the next port. It's possible to receive letters too, though in the modern communications age, few people feel the need.

Public holidays

These are too numerous to list on a per country basis. In Christian countries, Christmas (25 December), Easter (March or April) and New Year's Day (1 January) and the days either side of them may be designated public holidays. Ramadan (a month of fasting during daylight hours) and Eid ul-Adha, both based on the lunar calendar, are the main Islamic festivals.

Smoking

The majority of cruise ships place heavy restrictions on smoking. Restaurants are likely to be entirely smoke-free; cabins may be too. Smokers can usually light up on certain decks and in certain bars. On shore, habits and laws vary from one country to another.

Suggested reading and media

Before you go, cruise guides such as this one delve deep into the minutiae of cruising. Your best source of on-board information will be the daily newsletter that most ships post to their passengers' cabins each evening, which contains details of ship activities as well as the next day's port. Some ships may broadcast a live television feed to enable you to keep up to date with the news. To get you in the mood, nautical fiction runs the gamut from Herman Melville's demanding symbolic novel *Moby-Dick* to a range of easy-reading Mediterranean murder mysteries.

Tax

Some governments and port authorities impose a head tax on passengers for use of the port, but this will be already factored into the cost of your trip.

Telephones

Direct-dial satellite systems allow you to make phone calls from your cabin – although when you see the charges (around £4–£6 a minute) you're unlikely to want to. The satellite system transmits a mobile signal sometimes, and when you're docked or close to the land, your mobile phone will have reception from the national operators.

Time

The majority of countries covered here are on Central European time, which is one hour ahead of the UK, six ahead of New York and eight hours behind Sydney. Exceptions are Portugal, Morocco and Algeria (an hour behind the main group), and Greece, Turkey, Cyprus and Egypt (an hour ahead). Times may vary by an hour in winter.

Toilets

Ship washrooms are kept clean and well stocked. When you get off the ship, however, anything goes – be prepared for the dreaded squat toilet in some countries. Some businesses impose a small charge for use of the loos.

Travellers with disabilities

The orderly environment of the cruise can be an ideal way for a traveller with disabilities to get around the region. All ships have a few dedicated cabins (which can sell out quickly, so it's worth booking ahead), and some have made further adaptations (Braille signage in lifts and text telephones in cabins). Pick your vessel carefully. In general, the newer the ship is, the better it will accommodate travellers with disabilities – some cruises even cater entirely for the disabled market. You may want to avoid too many ports where disembarkation is by tender (small boats shuttling passengers to and from the anchored ship). This can be difficult, even for the able-bodied, and in some cases impossible for people with limited mobility.

Emergencies

The general emergency signal on a cruise ship consists of seven short blasts followed by one long one on the ship's alarm system. Specific instructions for what to do are given in the obligatory safety drill that takes place on the first night or morning of your holiday. Upon hearing the alarm, you should dress in warm clothes, retrieve your life jacket and go to your designated muster station. The safety briefing also sets out what you should do in various emergency situations (e.g. shouting 'man overboard' and alerting a crew member if you spot someone jump or fall over the side). In any other emergency, inform a member of staff or, if appropriate, activate the nearest alarm.

Medical facilities and insurance

All ships have a doctor and medical centre on board, although his or her services can be costly. This sum would pale into insignificance, though, beside the costs of getting you to land if you were taken seriously ill at sea, and taking out adequate insurance is essential. Indeed some cruise liners ask for your insurer's contact details. EHIC holders should take their card with them.

Risks

Although being at sea can increase your feeling of vulnerability, cruising is, in fact, statistically the safest form of transport in the travel industry. Under international law, crew members must be trained before they begin their employment. It's practically impossible to go over the side unless you choose to mount the rail. Fire is a risk, but the ship will have adequate detection and control systems in place. In the event of a fire, low-level lighting will lead you to the nearest emergency exit, but cautious travellers may wish to memorise the route, counting the number of doors and so on, in advance.

Outbreaks of food poisoning and the norovirus occasionally hit the

Emergency equipment on deck

One of Barcelona's motorbike policemen

headlines, but these are rare. Seasickness is also unlikely, as most ships are large and remain stable on the usually calm Mediterranean waters. Some add subaquatic flaps to minimise lurching. However, there is always the possibility of listing in rough weather, and passengers should take care, making use of handrails if necessary, when moving around the craft.

Police, safety and crime

Crime is extremely rare on cruise ships, as everyone's identity is known and staff members are well vetted before being hired. If you do become a victim, alert a member of staff, who will in turn inform the relevant authorities (which will depend on the location of

the ship, scene of crime and nationalities of those involved). If the crime is of sufficient seriousness, police from your home country will sometimes investigate it too.

In the more cosmopolitan ports, disembarking passengers will soon blend in with the social mix. However, in poorer countries where tourists are more likely to stand out in looks and dress from the local population, you will be identifiable to potential rogues as someone with little experience of your new milieu. There is no need for paranoia, but going from the protected environment of the cruise ship to the shore requires an adjustment of outlook: simply take as much care as you would in any new place or country.

Directory

Price guide

Prices are given for a three-course meal for one person, without drinks.

★	Budget
★★	Moderate
★★★	Moderately expensive
★★★★	Top end

IBERIA AND THE BALEARICS
Lisbon, Portugal
EATING OUT
Solar dos Bicos ★★★
A little overpriced, perhaps, and some of the waiters could do with a stint at charm school, but Solar dos Bicos offers ocean views, quaint atmosphere and decent Portuguese fare. Popular with tourists.
Rua dos Bacalhoeiros, 8A–8B, Alfama. Tel: (21) 886 9447. Open: Tue–Sun 8am–midnight.

Seville, Spain
EATING OUT
Corral del Agua ★/★★
The historical building – a renovated 18th-century palace – marble fountain and charming garden make a delightful backdrop to the food, which is traditional Andalusian with a modern twist. If you're brave enough, go for the bull's tail.
Callejón del Agua 6, Santa Cruz. Tel: (95) 422 4841. www.andalunet.com/corral-agua (Spanish only). Open: Mon–Sat noon–4pm & 8pm–midnight. Closed: Sun, plus Jan & Feb.

ENTERTAINMENT
La Carbonería
It may at times feel a little touristy, but visiting Seville without experiencing a flamenco show is akin to going to London and not getting on a double-decker bus.
Calle Levies 18, at junction with Calle Vidrio. Tel: (95) 421 4460. Show starts late evening. Free admission.

Gibraltar
EATING OUT
Thyme ★★★
The ever-changing bistro menu, which combines fresh ingredients in trendy international fusion dishes, is the main draw at this upmarket eatery, whose design was inspired by the contemporary London restaurant scene. The cocktail bar and open kitchen add to the atmosphere.
5 Cornwall's Lane. Tel: (200) 49199. www.dineatthyme.com. Open: Mon–Fri noon–3pm & 7.30pm–midnight, Sat 7pm–late. Closed: Sun.

Málaga, Spain
EATING OUT
Bar Logueno ★★
Legendary local eatery with no fewer than 75 different tapas on offer,

this bar is always packed. Considering the level of trade, service is fast and friendly.
Calle Marín García 9.
Tel: (95) 222 3048.
Open: Mon–Sat 1–4.30pm & 8pm–midnight.
Closed: Sun.

Valencia, Spain
EATING OUT
La Riuà ★★
A plethora of fish dishes – including exotic options like eel and octopus, along with other Spanish and Portuguese favourites – is on the menu at this place, in Valencia's historical centre. The ceramics on the walls make a pretty backdrop to your meal. La Riuà's popularity makes it worth booking a table.
Calle del Mar 27, just off Plaza de la Reina.
Tel: (96) 391 4571.
Open: Mon 2–4pm, Tue–Sat 2–4pm & 9–11pm. Closed: Sun.

ENTERTAINMENT
Café de las Horas
Baroque-style decor, such as chandeliers and velvet curtains,

make this an enjoyably plush environment in which to spend an evening.
Calle Conde de Almodóvar, off the Plaza de la Virgen.
Tel: (96) 391 7336.
Open: 9am–midnight.

Barcelona, Spain
EATING OUT
Taller de Tapas ★★
Serving tapas to tourists, this place is so popular you're likely to have to wait at the bar for a table. The outside seating is particularly sought after in good weather. Service can be hit and miss, but the high quality of the food is likely to compensate. There are three other outlets throughout the city.
Rambla Catalunya 49–51, Eixample.
Tel: (93) 487 4842.
www.tallerdetapas.com.
Open: Mon–Sat 7.30–1am, Sun noon–1am.
Restaurante Can Solé ★★★★
In business for over a century, this place is a fisherman's cottage on the outside, elegantly understated eatery on

the inside. The highly rated seafood has garnered many high-profile fans, some of whom are pictured on the walls. Be prepared to dig deep in your pocket.
Carrer Sant Carles 4.
Tel: (93) 221 5012. www. restaurantcansole.com.
Open: Tue–Sat 1.30–4pm & 8–11pm, Sun 1.30–4pm. Closed for two weeks in Aug.

ENTERTAINMENT
Gran Teatre del Liceu
Opera, dance, concerts and recitals are staged at this historical venue (it first opened in 1847), one of Spain's top opera houses.
La Rambla 51–9.
Tel: (93) 485 9998.
www.liceubarcelona.com

SPORT AND LEISURE
FC Barcelona
Footie fans will want to take in the famous Camp Nou stadium, home to one of the world's greatest football clubs. The club offers stadium tours, but of course the amazing atmosphere is best

appreciated at a game. Tickets can be bought online or by phone.
Camp Nou, Avinguda Aristides Maillol. Tel: (93) 496 3600. www.fcbarcelona.cat

Ibiza, Spain
EATING OUT
Can Caus
With its own farm out back, responsible for the provenance of some of the ingredients served up, anyone who's fussy about food miles will be in heaven at Can Caus. Relaxed and understandably popular.
3–5 Carretera Santa Gertrudis, km 3.5, Santa Gertrudis. Tel: (971) 197 516. www.campoibiza. com. Open: daily 11am– 4pm & 6pm–midnight.

ENTERTAINMENT
Amnesia
Home of the legendary Manumission club night, which it poached from rival super-club Privilege, and Cream.
San Rafel. Tel: (971) 198 041. www.amnesia.es
Privilege
The biggest club in the world, or so it claims,

this mega-club boasts a swimming pool and a 25m- (82ft-) high roof. Top-name DJs spin techno, house and electronica to crowds of up to 10,000 hedonists.
San Rafel. Tel: (971) 198 160. www.privilegeibiza.com. Admission charge.

Mallorca, Spain
EATING OUT
Café La Lonja ★★
This Palma stalwart has been designed to look like a turn-of-the-century inn. Tapas feature on the seasonal menu, alongside various snacks such as baguettes, sandwiches and salads. There is also a decent cocktail list. Dine inside or on the terrace.
Carrer Lonja del Mar 2, Palma. Tel: (971) 722 799. Open: Mon–Sat 10am–2am. Closed: Sun.

FRANCE, ITALY AND THEIR ISLANDS
Marseille, France
EATING OUT
Etienne ★★
This popular, buzzing pizzeria is a local institution. As well as

pizza, fresh from the wood-burning oven, there are plenty of other Marseille delicacies to whet your appetite. And your appetite had better be huge because the portions certainly will be. Credit cards are not accepted.
34 rue Lorette. No phone. Open: daily noon–2pm & 7.30–11.30pm.

ENTERTAINMENT
La Caravelle
The balcony of this renowned piano bar is the perfect place to watch the sun go down over Vieux Port. In a city that can sometimes seem a little rough around the edges, La Caravelle provides a touch of sophistication. Or you could just go for the free snacks, served with the aperitifs between 6 and 9pm.
34 quai Port. Tel: (491) 903 664. Open: daily 7pm–2am.

St-Tropez, France
EATING OUT
La Table du Marché ★★/★★★
Sushi and live music feature at this ultra-

trendy eatery, part of a chain from Christophe Leroy, the celebrity chef. The regional fare on offer is as delectable as you'd expect. A tea room adds to the urbane feel.

38 rue Georges Clemenceau.
Tel: (494) 978 520.
www.christophe-leroy.com (French only). Open: 7.30am–11.30pm.

Bar du Port ★★★

By day a laidback seafront restaurant where you can watch the St-Tropezians strut up and down by the sea, at night this place turns into a pre-club bar for the smart set, with a DJ. There are several decent pasta dishes on the menu, plus superb mussels.

7 quai Suffren.
Tel: (494) 970 054.
Open: daily noon–2.30am.

Cannes, France
EATING OUT
Le Petit Lardon ★★

Small and invariably busy, the Provençal and Burgundian fare on offer here has won more fans than this family-run restaurant can cater for.

Fish soup, snails, duck and rabbit are among the highlights.

3 rue Batéguier.
Tel: (493) 390 628. Open: Tue–Sun 7–10.30 or 11pm.

La Cave ★★/★★★

La Cave's unpretentious interior (think wooden chairs and chalkboard menus) seems rather at odds with the ostentatious Cannes vibe, but it's popular with locals and tourists alike.

9 boulevard de la République.
Tel: (493) 997 987. www. restaurant-lacave.com. Open: daily noon–2pm & 7–11pm.

Le Melaudy ★★★

Fabulous food and friendly staff make Le Melaudy a good choice. Fish dishes abound.

22 rue du Commandant André. Tél: (493) 392 137. Email: restaurantmelaudy @wanadoo.fr. Open: noon–3pm & 7–10 or 10.30pm. Closed: Mon.

Nice, France
EATING OUT
Le Café de Turin ★★★

A century of trade has made this Nice's top venue for shellfish. The

location is pretty, under the arcades of Place Garibaldi.

5 place Garibaldi.
Tel: (493) 622 952.
www.cafedeturin.com (French only). Open daily 8am–11pm.

Monte-Carlo, Monaco
EATING OUT
Café de Paris ★★/★★★

Right outside the casino, this is a great spot for watching the comings and goings of the nefarious denizens of Monaco. With a *belle époque* aspect, the restaurant serves up French and international cuisine. There is also a casino, which caters for people who don't meet the dress code for the main one, or who resent the entrance fee.

Place du Casino.
Tel: (0377) 9216 2000.
www.montecarlocasinos. com. Open: 8am–3am.

Le Louis XV ★★★★

Dining doesn't get much more upmarket than this three Michelin-starred Alain Ducasse restaurant. The menu is described as a 'Mediterranean

symphony', and a small army of staff will tend to your every need.
Hôtel de Paris, Place du Casino. Tel: (0377) 9806 8864. www.alain-ducasse.com. Open Thur–Mon 12.15–1.45pm & 8–9.45pm; also Jun–Sept Wed 12.15–1.45pm. Closed: Dec & two weeks in Feb.

Corsica, France
EATING OUT
Le 20123 ★★
Wonderfully traditional bistro that is an exact replica of the owner's old restaurant in his village (from whose postcode this place gets its unusual name). The food is equally traditional, with fresh ingredients fashioned into good old rustic dishes.
2 rue Roi de Rome, Ajaccio. Tel: (495) 215 005. www.20123.fr (French only). Open: Tue–Sun 7.30–11pm. Closed: Mon.

Sardinia, Italy
EATING OUT
T Restaurant ★★/★★★
Bright, chic and contemporary, this hotel restaurant draws on seasonal ingredients to put together Sardinian- and Mediterranean-inspired cuisine. Traditional Sardinian fresh-fish bouillabaisse and asparagus, saffron and dentex fish risotto are among the gastronomic highlights.
Via dei Giudicati, Cagliari. Tel: (070) 47400. www.thotel.it. Open: daily 7.30–10.30pm.

Genoa, Italy
EATING OUT
Da Domenico ★★
Received wisdom's guarantee of a restaurant's quality – whether it's popular with the locals – augurs well for Da Domenico. It's a private and intimate venue where meat and fish dishes are the order of the day. Book ahead if you don't want to be turned away.
Piazza Leonardo 3, Molo. Tel: (010) 540 289. Open: 10am–midnight. Closed: Mon.

ENTERTAINMENT
Teatro Stabile di Genova
One of several theatres in the city, this venue plays host to performances by the Genoa Theatre Company.
Piazza Borgo Pila 42. Tel: (010) 534 2212. www.teatrostabilegenova.it (Italian only).

Teatro Carlo Felice
Genoa's top opera house also stages ballet, concerts and recitals. It was built in 1826 on the site of a Dominican church (after the monks were summarily ousted). Its interior, though, is modern, after British shelling and looters between them destroyed the original rococo ceiling.
Piazza De Ferrari. Tel: (010) 538 1223. www.carlofelice.it

Livorno, Italy
ENTERTAINMENT
Arena Ardenza
One of three open-air cinemas in Livorno operating throughout the summer. Language issues may limit your understanding (unless you're fluent in Italian!), but the experience of watching a film al fresco is still an enjoyable one. Films change daily, beginning every night at

9.30pm (tickets on sale from 9pm).
Piazza Sforzini, Ardenza. Tel: (050) 502640.

Florence, Italy
EATING OUT
Trattoria La Madia ★★/★★★
With chequered red and white tablecloths, exposed stonework and art on the wall, this fifty-year-old eatery is exactly how an Italian trattoria should look and feel. Enjoy the warm atmosphere as you tuck into the quintessence of Italian cuisine.
Via del Giglio 14. Tel: (055) 218 563. Open: daily noon–3.30pm & 6.30–11pm.

ENTERTAINMENT
Teatro Comunale
Concerts, opera, dance and theatre take centre stage at Florence's main venue for the performing arts. The theatre also plays host to the annual *Maggio Musicale Fiorentino*, which in fact runs from around April through to June, despite the timeframe its name suggests (*maggio* means May).
Corso Italia 16.

Tel: (055) 2779 350. www. maggiofiorentino.com. Box office open: daily 10am–6pm.

Rome, Italy
EATING OUT
Pizzeria Baffetto ★
Held by many Romans to offer the best pizza in the city, Pizzeria Baffetto is justifiably popular, so if you're the impatient kind (or very hungry), you might want to avoid waiting by arriving early. Neither reservations nor credit cards are accepted.
Via del Governo Vecchio 114, near Piazza Navona & the Pantheon. Tel: (06) 686 1617. Open: daily 6.30pm–1am. Closed: 12–31 Aug. Bus: 46, 62, 64.

Dal Bolognese ★★★
Join the throngs of Rome's beautiful people grappling for the outside tables at this fine restaurant, which certainly lives up to its impressive reputation. The food is not experimental, just Italian favourites from the region done very, very well. And there is no need

to feel unadventurous if you go for the eponymous sauce.
Piazza del Popolo 1–2, near the Spanish Steps. Tel: (06) 361 1426. Open: Tue–Sun 1–3pm & 8.15pm–midnight. Closed: Mon and 20 days in August. Metro: Flaminio.

ENTERTAINMENT
Teatro dell'Opera di Roma
Opera, ballet and concerts are staged at this historic venue, which also offers visitors guided tours.
Piazza Beniamino Gigli 7. Tel: (06) 481 601. www.operaroma.it. Metro: Repubblica Teatro dell'Opera.

Sicily, Italy
EATING OUT
Trattoria Altri Tempi ★★
Restaurants don't get much more traditional than this family-run trattoria, which emanates old-school hospitality. Rustic barrels, decorative bottles of wine and simple wooden furniture add to the country vibe, and the food is suitably local.

*Via Sammartino 65–7,
Palermo.
Tel: (091) 323 480.
www.trattoriaaltritempi.it.
Open: 12.30–3pm &
8–11.30pm.
Closed: Sun in Jul & Aug
and 12 Aug–10 Sept.*

ENTERTAINMENT
Greek-Roman Theatre
Part of the ancient Greek
colony of Tyndaris, the
theatre enjoys a splendid
spot up above the
Tyrrhenian Sea. While
the theatre can be visited
as part of the site during
the day, attending one of
the plays or shows staged
during the summer
season will afford a
better glimpse into the
venue's vivid past.
*Zona Archeologica,
Tyndaris, Messina.
Tel: (0921) 421 547.
www.regione.sicilia.it
(Italian).*

Venice, Italy
EATING OUT
Ristorante Giorgione ★
Dine on hearty Venetian
and Italian cuisine, with
an emphasis on the
piscatorial, to the strains
of owner Lucio, who
provides nightly live

music. Famous
customers have included
Rolling Stone Ronnie
Wood and Germany's
former chancellor
Gerhard Schröder.
It's a little out of the
way, but the warm
welcome and bargain
prices make this place
worth seeking out.
*Via Garibaldi 1533,
Sestiere di Castello.
Tel: (041) 522 8727.
www.ristorantegiorgione.it.
Open: Thur–Tue
noon–3.30pm & 6–10pm.*
Trattoria da Fiore ★★★
Unlike the majority of
Venice's tourist eateries,
which are high on cost
and low on quality, this
relaxed and homely
place serves a range of
enjoyable food, with the
fish a highlight.
*Calle delle Botteghe, near
Piazza San Marco.
Tel: (041) 523 5310.
Open: Wed–Mon
noon–3pm & 7–10pm.*

ENTERTAINMENT
Teatro La Fenice
The name of this opulent
theatre translates as
'Phoenix Theatre', and
the venue today stands
after several fires

devastated previous
structures. The design of
the auditorium is a copy
of how it was in the
19th century; though it
angered purists, it is
undeniably striking.
*Campo San Fantin, San
Marco. Tel: (041) 2424.
www.teatrolafenice.it
(Italian only).
Call centre open: daily
7.30am–8pm.*

DALMATIAN COAST, GREECE AND TURKEY
Split, Croatia
EATING OUT
Makro Vega ★
Clean, bright and
modern, Makro Vega's
vegetarian and vegan fare
is a welcome change
from Split's many
identikit pizza
restaurants. The menu
changes daily, and the set
menu is great value.
Desserts (which come
highly recommended),
snacks and main meals
can be taken away. Soft
drinks only.
*Leština 2. Tel: (21) 394
440. www.makrovega.hr
(Croatian only).
Open: Mon–Fri 9am–
7pm, Sat 9am–5pm.
Closed: Sun.*

Dubrovnik, Croatia
EATING OUT

Poklisar ★★

Enjoy some Croatian and Dalmatian seafood (or pizza if you're feeling less adventurous) overlooking the city's harbour. Nightly live music and an attractive terrace add to the atmosphere.
Ribarnika 1.
Tel: (20) 322 176.
www.poklisar.com. Open: daily 9am–midnight.

Corfu, Greece
EATING OUT

Rex Restaurant ★★

A family restaurant in operation since 1932 (albeit with a few different families at the helm over the years), in one of Corfu's busier areas. The extensive menu combines perennial Italian favourites with Greek classics like moussaka and tzatziki. Choose between a terrace table and one inside the historical building.
Kapodistriou 66, Corfu Town. Tel: (26610) 39649; www.restaurantrex.gr. Open: daily noon–midnight.

SPORT AND LEISURE

Achilleon Diving Centre

Equipment hire for experienced divers and tuition for novices.
Ermones Bay.
Tel: (26610) 95350.
www.diving-corfu.com

Zante, Greece
SPORT AND LEISURE

Vasilikos Zakynthos Water Sports Centre

All manner of aquatic pastimes are on offer here, from high-octane thrills such as paragliding, water skiing, jet skiing, banana boating and ringo rides to pedaloes and canoes. (Service can vary at beachside watersports operators so it's always best to make enquiries and get current recommendations before booking.)
Vasilikos.
Tel: (26950) 35325/6/7/8.
Email: stnicks@otenet.gr.

Athens, Greece
EATING OUT

Athinaikon ★★

Tourists are thin on the ground at this traditional *ouzeri*, which caters in the main to the local office workers. Dine either on *mezedes* (a selection of appetisers) or order a main course; prices run the gamut. Old photos on the wall and a pleasant decor add to the ambience.
2 Themistokleous, near Plateia Omonia.
Tel: (210) 383 8485.
Open: Mon–Sat 11am–midnight. Closed: Sun & much of Aug.

Kuzina ★★

Stylish and chic, contemporary Kuzina delivers traditional ingredients with a fusion twist. There are hints of both the Mediterranean and the Far East among the delectable fare. Meals can be taken at a pavement table or on the terrace overlooking the Acropolis. Or dine inside the bright and modish bar area.
Adrianou 9, Thissio.
Tel: (210) 324 0133.
Open: 1pm–2am.

ENTERTAINMENT

Dora Stratou Dance Company

With a 50-year history, this dance company stages nightly folk

performances (except Mondays) during the summer season at an open-air theatre.
Philopappou Hill, opposite the Acropolis. Tel: (210) 324 4395. www.grdance.org. Metro: Acropolis, Theseion. Bus: 15.

Paros, Greece
 EATING OUT
Taverna Akrogiali ★/★★
This family-run restaurant is one of Paros's treasures. Friendly, personal service and a superb terrace overlooking the sea both work in its favour, but the main draw is the superb food, simple local dishes done to perfection. Desserts are on the house. Customers invariably leave well fed and happy.
Livadia, Parikia. Tel: (22840) 21319. Open: 8.30am–1 or 2am (Easter–Oct).

Mykonos, Greece
ENTERTAINMENT
Cavo Paradiso
The cream of international DJs – Carl Cox, Sasha, David

Morales, Frankie Knuckles and Armin van Buuren among them – have done sets at this cliff-top club, whose location throws some excellent views into the mix.
Above Paradise Beach, Mykonos Town. Tel: (22890) 27205. www.cavoparadiso.gr
Pierro's
One of the top gay clubs on Mykonos, which is itself a Mecca for gay travellers. Pierro's promises 'wild parties, great music, drag shows, and a joyous atmosphere'. It's also known as 'the square', due to the several other venues in the vicinity.
Odos Matoyanni, Mykonos Town. Tel: (22890) 22177. www.pierrosbar.gr

Syros, Greece
EATING OUT
Egripo ★
This taverna has charming sea views and simple decor. The seasonal menu is Greek traditional, with a significant piscatorial element, due to the location.
Azolimnos.

Tel: (22810) 61005. www.egripo.com. Open: Thur–Sat noon–4am & Sun 11am–late afternoon.

Istanbul, Turkey
EATING OUT
Balıkçı Sabahattin ★★
Family-run fish restaurant with an impressive heritage, occupying a refurbished Ottoman house. There's a cobblestone terrace outside. Appetisers are brought to the table, but menus are also provided. The service here gets good reviews. Past diners include Jean Paul Gaultier. Sultanahmet has a plethora of high-quality restaurants, many with pleasant roof terraces.
Cankurtaran, Sultanahmet (behind Armada Hotel), Eminonu. Tel: (212) 458 1824. www. balikcisabahattin.com. Open: noon–3pm & 7–10.30pm.
Changa ★★★
Istanbul dining doesn't get much trendier than Changa. This acclaimed fusion restaurant occupies a century-old Art Nouveau townhouse.

In a town with its fair share of good eateries, it's easy to detect the hand of an international chef. The exquisitely presented food includes main courses such as wasabi and salmon tortellini, and grilled loin of lamb with roasted quince. The glass-ceilinged basement kitchen is another highlight.
Siraselviler Caddesi 87/1, Taksim. Tel: (212) 249 1348. www.changa-istanbul.com. Open: Mon–Sat 12.30–3pm & 7pm–2am. Closed: Sun.

SPORT AND LEISURE
Çemberlitaş Hamamı
As essential an Istanbul experience as drinking a revitalising fresh orange juice is a trip to a Turkish bathhouse, or hammam.
Çemberlitaş Hamamı is recommended as a good introduction to what can, initially, be a little unnerving: namely the most intensive massage you've ever had. In attractive and historical environs you will be pummelled and pounded across the pain barrier – and come out feeling utterly invigorated.
8 Vezirhan Caddesi, Çemberlitaş. Tel: (212) 522 7974. www.cemberlitashamami.com.tr. Open: daily 6am–midnight.

Bodrum, Turkey
EATING OUT
Yağhane ★★
Dine among Bodrum's yacht lovers at this popular eatery whose home is a 19th-century olive oil factory. The Mediterranean fare and the warm service both get plaudits. Dining is under the stars; sit at the edge if you want to watch the marina's comings and goings while you eat.
Neyzen Tevfik Caddesi 170, Bodrum Marina. Tel: (252) 313 4747. www.yaghanebodrum.com. Open: daily 10.30am–midnight.

Marmaris, Turkey
EATING OUT
Liman ★★
Bustling local stalwart, thanks in part to its location inside the bazaar. Seafood features prominently among the highlights, with the fish soup and casserole particular favourites. The *mezes* are also popular. It's not the cheapest place, but offers good value.
40 Sokak 38. Tel: (252) 412 6336. Open: daily 8.30am–1am.

Antalya, Turkey
EATING OUT
Marina Restaurant ★★/★★★
This upmarket French eatery, part of the Marina Hotel, ranks among the resort's best. It is divided into two parts, one in the main building and the other in the garden. All sorts of international flavours have been drawn upon in the concoction of the sublime dishes on offer, including Iranian caviar and Madagascan sauce.
Mermerli Sokak 15, Kaleiçi. Tel: (242) 247 5490. Open: noon–11pm.

Kos, Greece
EATING OUT
Sagittarius ★★
Now twenty years old, Sagittarius remains a

popular Kos eatery. The wide-ranging menu encompasses Greek, Indian and Italian fare, with international favourites such as pizza and pasta, curry and some vegetarian options. There is also a children's menu. Portions are generous, while service and setting help generate repeat custom.
Tigaki. Tel: (22420) 69096. www.sagittariuskos.com. Open: daily 9am–midnight (May–Oct).

Rhodes, Greece
EATING OUT
Alexis Taverna ★★★★
A galaxy of illustrious figures, including Winston Churchill and Jackie O, has dined at this family concern over its half-century of business, but the fish is the real star of the show. Vegetables are sourced from the restaurant's own organic greenhouse. It's not cheap and, given the quality, nor should it be.
18 Sokratous, Rhodes Town. Tel: (241) 029 347. Open: May–Oct Mon–Sat 10am–4pm & 7pm–1am.

Crete, Greece
EATING OUT
Ippocampus ★
Traditional appetiser-style Greek dining is the idea at Ippocampus, and it's great value. This *ouzeri* draws mainly a local crowd, attracted by the bargain prices and great seafood. Dine inside or alfresco, on the pavement.
3 Mitsotaki, Iraklion. Tel: (821) 028 2081. Open: Mon–Fri 1–3.30pm & 7pm–midnight.

Cyprus
EATING OUT
La Maison Fleurie ★★★★
Don your glad rags for this highly acclaimed sumptuous French restaurant. The plush red-and-white-themed environs are in keeping with the posh nosh on offer. Outside dining is possible in summer. Reservations essential.
18 Christaki Kranou, Potamos Yermasoyias, Limassol. Tel: (25) 320 680. www. frenchrestaurantcyprus.com. Open: daily noon–3.30pm & 6pm–midnight.

ENTERTAINMENT
The Castle Club
Cyprus's biggest club (holding up to 3,000 revellers) has three rooms, and hosts a variety of themed nights, including Skool Disco, I Luv RnB and Stiletto Sunday. There's also an outside chill-out area. The place is pretty hard to miss – it's housed in a mock castle.
20–22 Louka Louka Street, Agia Napa. www.thecastleclub.com
Insomnia
Old-school house and garage attracting the late-night/early-morning crowd.
Nissi Beach Road, opposite McDonald's, Agia Napa. Tel: (3) 724 240. www.3ds.com.cy/insomnia. Open: 4–7am.

SPORT AND LEISURE
Crest Dive
PADI courses, one-off dives for beginners, snorkelling and adventure safaris are among the aquatic pursuits on offer. An affiliated company, **Crest Water Sports** (*www. crestwatersports.com*),

deals with the boat and jet-ski hire, water skiing, parasailing, wind surfing and watersports in general.

St Raphael Marina, 4520 Parekklisia, Old Limassol Nicosia Road, Limassol. Tel: (25) 634 076. Email: enquiries@crestdive.com. www.crestdive.com

THE SOUTH
Alexandria, Egypt
EATING OUT

Café Trianon ★★

It's not the cheapest place for a bite to eat, but when you see the swish environs you might not mind too much. The Trianon consists of a restaurant, café and patisserie, all of them decorated with fabulous artwork. The food also gets rave reviews, and the *om ali* (bread and butter pudding) is legendary.

Midan Saad Zaghlul (by the sea). Tel: (3) 4822 0986. Open: daily 10am–1am.

Valletta, Malta
EATING OUT

La Dolce Vita ★★

The split-level dining room exudes simple elegance, or you can sit outside on the terrace to enjoy the pretty bay views. Its fresh fish is particularly sought after, and there are also meat, pasta and vegetarian options. Be sure to call ahead and book.

159 St George's Road. Tel: 2133 7036. Open: 11am–11pm.

ENTERTAINMENT

Teatru Manoel

Dating back to 1732, Malta's oldest theatre is also one of the most long-standing in Europe. Opera, ballet, modern dance, music, children's performances and drama are on the programme.

115 Old Theatre Street. Tel: 2124 6389. www.teatrumanoel.com. mt. Box office open: Mon–Fri 9am–1pm & 5–7pm, Sat 9am–1pm.

Tunis, Tunisia
EATING OUT

Dar el-Jeld ★★★★

Get your glad rags on for a visit to this place, held by many to be the country's best eatery. Housed in an upscale townhouse, Dar el-Jeld is an impossibly glamorous throwback to another era, with 18th-century tiles, live sitar music, smart old-school waiters and a clientele that resembles the cast of *Casablanca*. The national cuisine at its best.

5–10 rue Dar el Jeld. Tel: (71) 560 916. Open: Mon–Sat 12.30–3pm & 8pm–midnight.

Tangier, Morocco
EATING OUT

El Korsan ★★

The Moroccan restaurant at the El Minzah Hotel is one of Tangier's most opulent. Done out in rich Moorish reds with drapes, the exotic atmosphere is sometimes enhanced by a traditional dancer who wends her way around the tables. Local specialities include tajine of young pigeon stewed with pears and honey and couscous with seven vegetables. There is also an international menu.

85 rue de la Liberté. Tel: (39) 935 885. www.elminzah.com. Open: daily 8–11pm.

Index

Acknowledgements

Thomas Cook Publishing wishes to thank VASILE SZAKACS for the photographs in this book, to whom the copyright belongs, except for the following images:

ARCHIVE OF THE TOURIST BOARD OF THE PROVINCE OF VENICE 83, 85
DREAMSTIME.COM Preckas 1, Onefivenine 9, Dbajurin 19, Michael Corrigan 34, Cristian Nitu 47, Ferdericb 56, Reinhold Einsiedler 62, Uwe Blosfeld 74, Bryan Busovicki 75, Alexandre Fagundes De Fagundes 78, Saba11 80, Andre Nantel 89, Nigel Monckton 93, Pavel Buran 94, Vitaly Titov 110
DUBROVNIK TOURIST BOARD 88
FLICKR/joaoa 30, pm.raymon 32, *hoodrat* 64, Eric Perrone 66, dullhunk 91, zoonabar 96, phileole 115
IBIZA TRAVEL 42, 43, 46
MOROCCO TOURISM 126
PICTURES COLOUR LIBRARY 63, 79, 86, 121, 124, 131
TURESPAÑA 31, 35, 36, 37, 45
TURISMO DE LISBOA (www.visitlisboa.com) 27, 28
VISITCYPRUS.COM 117
VISITSPLIT.COM 87
WIKIMEDIA COMMONS/Diliff 70, 71, Dedda71 81, Jastrow 90, Dr. K 92, Gérard Janot 114, AVIAD BUBLIL 116
WORLD PICTURES/PHOTOSHOT 51, 77, 111, 113, 119, 123, 132

For CAMBRIDGE PUBLISHING MANAGEMENT LTD:
Project editor: Rosalind Munro
Copy editor: Penny Isaac
Typesetter: Paul Queripel
Proofreader: Catherine Burch
Indexer: Karolin Thomas

SEND YOUR THOUGHTS TO
BOOKS@THOMASCOOK.COM

We're committed to providing the very best up-to-date information in our travel guides and constantly strive to make them as useful as they can be. You can help us to improve future editions by letting us have your feedback. If you've made a wonderful discovery on your travels that we don't already feature, if you'd like to inform us about recent changes to anything that we do include, or if you simply want to let us know your thoughts about this guidebook and how we can make it even better – we'd love to hear from you.

Send us ideas, discoveries and recommendations today and then look out for your valuable input in the next edition of this title.

Emails to the above address, or letters to Travellers Series Editor, Thomas Cook Publishing, PO Box 227, Coningsby Road, Peterborough PE3 8SB, UK.

Please don't forget to let us know which title your feedback refers to!